D1084743

SAMSON

A secret betrayed, a vow ignored

JAMES L. CRENSHAW

JOHN KNOX PRESS
ATLANTA

Library of Congress Cataloging in Publication Data

Crenshaw, James L
  Samson: a secret betrayed, a vow ignored.

  Bibliography: p.
  Includes indexes.
  1. Bible. O.T. Judges XIII, 1–XVI, 31—Criticism, interpretation, etc.
2. Samson, Judge of Israel. 3. Riddles—History and criticism.
BS1305.2.c73   222'.32'077   77–15748
ISBN 0–8042–0170–6

Preface

For several years I have been interested in riddles. Their peculiar power to communicate on two levels simultaneously intrigues me, inasmuch as my own task as a teacher of the Hebrew Scriptures must be carried on before two entirely different audiences—beginning students and learned colleagues. This fascination for riddles naturally led me to a study of the Samson narrative, and eventuated in the following attempt to stimulate the interest of novice and specialist at the same time. Those who are familiar with the vast literature dealing with Samson will find much here that they have seen before, and hopefully some wholly new perceptions. Others whose interests and experiences have not contained any exposure to the biblical story and its explication, will, I trust, find this book comprehensible.

I wish to thank The Society for Values in Higher Education for a Post Doctoral Cross Disciplinary Fellowship that enabled me to spend the academic year 1972–1973 in Heidelberg, Germany, where I studied folklore in general and riddles in particular, and the Research Council of Vanderbilt University for generous assistance on more than one occasion. In addition, I am especially grateful to Walter Harrelson, Toni Craven, and Kathe Pfisterer for reading the manuscript and offering many helpful suggestions.

More than seventeen years ago my wife and I watched our oldest son, James Timothy, begin to discover the world around him. His quest for knowledge from then until now compares favorably, I think, insofar as thrill and excitement are concerned, with any of the episodes recounted in the Samson narrative. In any event, I am grateful to have been a participant in that wonderful search, and wish to dedicate this book to Tim.

James L. Crenshaw
May 20, 1977

Contents

To Tim

Three Sacred Fonts

Sacred altar and holy table
  join the blessed font
in majestic invitational chant
  to which comes our twelve year old,
white robed, innocent,
  object of loving parents' gaze,
who press one another's hands
  and glance upon him and back again
where four founts beclouded
  pour forth droplets unchecked.

By what miracle cleansed,
  this impish son under water pure?
The same power of years ago
  that took another drop
lovingly placed in mute lips
  and from it shaped
this fruit of pleasure,
  gift of prayer,
can spread a rainbow,
  halo-like over these three fonts,
staying the cloudless rain
  until yet another day
when the miracle of the holiest font
  new life to him and an unknown her grant.

(1973)

A Translation of *Judges 13:1—16:31*

Now the Israelites kept on doing evil in the LORD's eyes, and he gave them into the hand of the Philistines for forty years. There was a man from Zorah belonging to the Danite clan whose name was Manoah. His wife was barren and had not given birth. Appearing to the woman, a messenger of the LORD said to her: "Lo, you are barren and have not given birth, but you will conceive and give birth to a son. Take care now that you do not drink wine or strong drink, or that you eat anything unclean. For, behold, you will conceive and give birth to a son, and no razor shall come upon his head, since the boy will be a Nazirite of God from the womb. He shall begin to deliver Israel from the hand of the Philistines."

Then the woman went to her husband and told him: "A man of God came to me, and his countenance was like the appearance of God's angel, exceedingly awesome. I did not ask him where he came from, and he did not tell me his name. He did say to me, 'Lo, you will conceive and bear a son, and now do not drink wine or strong drink and do not eat anything unclean. For the boy will be a Nazirite of God from the womb until the day of his death.'"

Then Manoah entreated the LORD: "O LORD, let the man of God whom you sent come again to us and teach us what we ought to do for the boy who will be born." Now God paid heed to Manoah's plea, and the angel of God came again to the woman. She was sitting in the field, and Manoah her husband was not with her. Quickly, the woman ran and told her husband: "Lo, the man who came to me on that day has appeared to me." Manoah got up, followed his wife, came to the man, and said to him: "Are you the man who spoke to this woman?" He said, "I am." Then Manoah said: "Now when your words come to be,[1] what will be the stipulation concerning the boy and his work?" The angel of the LORD said to Manoah: "From everything that I said to the woman, let her guard herself. From everything that proceeds from the vine—wine—she shall not eat; wine and strong drink she shall not drink and anything unclean she shall not eat. Everything that I commanded her, let her observe."

Manoah spoke to the angel of the LORD: "Let us detain you, and we will prepare a kid in your presence." Now the angel of the LORD said to Manoah: "Even if you detained me I would not eat any of your bread, but if you (wish to) make an offering to the LORD, let it ascend." For Manoah did not know that he was an angel of the LORD. And Manoah said to the LORD's angel: "Who . . . your name?[2]—When your words come to be so that we can honor you." The angel of the LORD said to him: "Why is this—you ask about my name?—for it is wonderful."[3]

Manoah took a kid and a cereal offering and sacrificed them upon the rock to the LORD and to the one doing marvels. Now Manoah and his wife were watching. As the flame from the altar went heavenward, the angel of the LORD ascended in the flame of the altar—now Manoah and his wife were watching, and fell upon their faces to the ground. The angel of the LORD did not again appear to Manoah and his wife. Then Manoah knew that he was the LORD's angel, and said to his wife: "We shall surely die, for we have seen God." But his wife said to him, "If the LORD had wanted to slay us he would not have accepted the burnt offering and cereal offering from our hand, nor would he have shown us all these things, nor would he have just now caused us to hear anything like this."

[1]Although many translators render this as jussive, "May your words come true," the syntax is unusual.
[2]The customary form is *mah,* not *mi.*
[3]Read *peli'.*

So the woman gave birth to a son, and she called his name Samson. The boy grew, and the LORD blessed him. Now the spirit of the LORD began to stir him in Mahaneh-dan between Zorah and Eshtaol.

Samson went down to Timnah and saw a woman in Timnah, one of the Philistines. Having gone up, he told his father and his mother: "I saw a woman in Timnah from the daughters of the Philistines. Now get her for me for a wife." His father and his mother said to him: "Is there not a woman among the daughters of your brothers and among all my people that you must take a wife from the uncircumcized Philistines?" But Samson said to his father: "Get her for me, for she is right in my eyes." Now his father and his mother did not know that it[4] was from the LORD, for he wished to seek (an affront) from the Philistines. At that time Philistines were ruling over Israel.

Accompanied by his father and mother, Samson went down to Timnah. He came to the vineyards of Timnah, and lo, a young lion came roaring to meet him. The spirit of the LORD seized him, and he tore it as one tears a kid, and nothing was in his hand. He did not tell his father and his mother what he had done. Having gone down, he spoke to the woman, and she was right in Samson's eyes. After some days he returned to take her, and he turned aside to look at the carcass of the lion. Lo, a swarm of bees was in the lion, and honey. Scraping it into his hand, he went, eating as he walked. When he came to his father and his mother, he gave them some and they ate, but he did not tell them he had taken the honey from the lion's carcass.

Now his father went down to the woman, and there Samson made a feast. For so the young men used to do. When they saw him,[5] they took thirty of their companions and they were with him. Samson said to them: "Let me pose a riddle for you; if you can actually tell it to me during the seven days of the feast, and

[4]Perhaps *hi'* refers to the woman—"she was from the LORD."

[5]Strong versional support for *b^eyir'atam* (because they feared him) exists (LXX A, Syr[h], OL).

find it out, then I shall give you thirty linen and thirty festal garments. But if you cannot tell me, *you* shall give me thirty linen and thirty festal garments." They said to him: "Pose your riddle that we may hear it." He said to them:

> Food came from the eater; sweetness came from strength.

And they were unable to declare the riddle during three days. On the seventh[6] day they said to Samson's wife: "Entice your husband and tell us the riddle, lest we burn you and your father's house with fire. Did you bring us to impoverish us, or not?" Samson's wife wept upon him and said, "You only hate me, you do not love me; you have put a riddle to my country-men, and you have not told it to me." He said to her, "Lo, I have not told my father or my mother, and I shall tell you?"[7] Now she wept before him the seven days of the feast, and on the seventh day he told her because she wearied him. Then she told the riddle to her countrymen. The men of the city said to him on the seventh day before he entered the chamber:[8]

> What is sweeter than honey, and what is stronger than a lion?

And he said to them:

> Had you not plowed with my heifer, you would not have found out my riddle.

The spirit of the LORD seized him, and he went down to Askelon, slew thirty men among them, took their tunics, and gave them to those who had declared the riddle. His anger burning, he went to his father's house. Samson's wife became the companion's, who was his "best man."

After some time Samson, accompanied by a kid, visited his

---

[6]Some versions read "fourth"; in verse 14, the word "third" appears, which differs from "sixth" in Hebrew by only one letter.

[7]The negative of the preceding verb may do double duty, hence "I shall not tell you."

[8]Read *hachadrah* (cf. 15:1).

wife during the wheat harvest. He said, "I shall go[9] to my wife in the inner chamber," but her father would not let him enter. Her father said, "I really thought that you actually hated her, and I gave her to your companion. Is not her younger sister better than she? Let her be for you instead." Samson said to them: "This time I am innocent with regard to the Philistines when I do them harm." Samson went away and captured three hundred foxes; he took torches, turned them tail to tail, and set a torch between each pair of tails. When he had kindled fire in the torches, he sent (them) into the Philistine's standing grain. It burned the shocks and standing grain, and even olive groves. The Philistines asked, "Who did this?" and were told, "Samson, the son-in-law of the Timnite; for he took his wife and gave her to his companion." The Philistines went up and burned her and her father[10] with fire. Then Samson said, "If you act like this, I swear that I shall be avenged upon you, and afterwards I shall quit." He smote them hip upon thigh, a great slaughter; then he went down and dwelt in a rocky crag at Etam.

The Philistines went up and encamped in Judah, and made a raid at Lehi. The people of Judah asked, "Why have you come up against us?" They answered, "We have come up to bind Samson, to do to him what he did to us." Three thousand men from Judah went down to the rock crag at Etam and said to Samson, "Do you not know that Philistines rule over us? Now what is this you have done to us?" He said to them, "Just as they did to me, so I did to them." They said to him, "We have come down to bind you in order to give you into the hand of the Philistines." Samson said to them, "Swear to me that you yourselves will not attack me." They said to him, "No. For we shall bind you tightly and give you into their hand, but we will not kill you." They bound him with two new ropes and took him up from the rock. He came to Lehi, and Philistines shouted against him. The LORD's spirit came upon him and the ropes upon his arms became like flax that people burn with fire, and his bonds

[9]Or jussive—"Let me go."
[10]Perhaps we should add "the house of" with LXX[AL], Syr[h], Syr.

melted from his hands. He found a fresh jawbone of an ass, reached and took it, and slew a thousand men with it. Then Samson said, "With the jawbone of the ass, ass upon asses, with the jawbone of the ass, I have slain a thousand men." When he finished speaking he discarded the jawbone and called the place "Ramath-lehi."[11]

Being exceedingly thirsty, he called to Yahweh and said, "You have given this great victory into the hand of your servant, but now I am about to die with thirst, and I shall fall into the hand of the uncircumcized." Then God split the hollow place that is at Lehi, and water flowed from it. He drank, his spirit returned, and he revived. Therefore he called its name En Haqqore',[12] which is in Lehi until this day. He judged Israel in the days of the Philistines twenty years.

Samson went down to Gaza and saw a woman there, a harlot, and he went in to her. Gazites were informed, "Samson has come here." Surrounding (the house), they lay in wait for him all night at the gate of the city. They kept quiet all night, thinking, "(Let us wait) until the light of morning, then we shall slay him." Samson lay until midnight, and arose in the middle of the night. Seizing the door to the city gate, together with the two posts, he pulled them up with the bar, put them on his shoulders, and took them up to the top of the mountain that is opposite Hebron.

Afterwards he loved a woman in the valley of Soreq. Her name was Delilah. Philistine lords went up to her and said to her, "Entice him and see in what way his strength is great, and in what way we may overpower him and bind him, to afflict him. We will each give you eleven hundred silver pieces. Then Delilah said to Samson, "Please tell me wherein your strength is great, and how you may be bound so as to afflict you." Samson said to her, "If they bind me with seven fresh bowstrings that have not been dried, then I shall become weak and I shall be like any other man." The Philistine lords brought to her seven

[11]Hill of the Jawbone.
[12]Spring of the Caller (Partridge).

fresh bowstrings that had not been dried, and she bound him with them. Now those lying in wait stayed in an inner chamber, and she said to him, "Philistines are upon you, Samson." He snapped the bowstrings as a string of flax snaps when it touches fire. Now his strength was not known. Delilah said to Samson, "Lo, you have mocked me; you have told me lies. Now tell me how you may be bound." He said to her, "If they bind me securely with new ropes with which no work has been done, then I shall become weak and be like another man." Delilah took new ropes, bound him with them, and said to him, "Philistines are upon you, Samson." Now those lying in wait stayed in the inner chamber. He broke them from upon his arms like a thread. Delilah said to Samson, "Until now you have mocked me and told me lies. Tell me how you may be bound." He said to her, "If you weave the seven locks on my head with the web . . . ."[13] She tightened it with the pin and said to him, "Philistines are upon you, Samson." He awoke from sleep and pulled away the pin, the loom, and the web. She said to him, "How can you say, 'I love you,' and your heart is not with me? These three times you have mocked me and have not told me in what way your strength is great." It happened that she pressed him with her words all the days; she vexed him, and his soul came short of dying. Then he told her all his heart. He said to her, "A razor has never gone upon my head, for I have been a Nazirite of God from my mother's womb. If I am shaven, then my strength will leave me and I shall be weak, and become like every man." When Delilah saw that he had told her all his heart, she sent and summoned the Philistine lords, saying "Come up at once, for he has told me all his heart." The Philistine lords came up to her and brought silver in their hands. When she had caused him to sleep on her knees, she called to a man and he shaved[14] the seven locks of his head. Then she began to afflict him, and his strength had departed from him. She said, "Philistines are

[13]The Hebrew text has lost several words; they have probably been preserved in LXX^B.
[14]The Massoretic Text has, "She shaved."

upon you, Samson." Awaking from sleep, he said, "I shall go forth this time as before, and shake myself free." He did not know that the LORD had departed from him.

The Philistines seized him, gouged out his eyes, and took him down to Gaza. They bound him with bronze chains, and he became a grinder in the house of his captors.[15] But the hair of his head began to grow after it had been cut.

Philistine lords assembled to sacrifice a great sacrifice to Dagon, their god, and to rejoice. They said, "Our god has given into our hands Samson our enemy." When the people saw him they praised their god, for they said, "Our god has given our enemy into our hands, and the ravager of our land who has killed many of us." When their heart was merry, they said, "Call Samson that he may make sport for us." They called Samson from the house of imprisonment, and he made sport before them. They stood him between the pillars, and Samson said to the lad who was holding him by the hand, "Lead me and let me feel the pillars upon which the house rests, that I may lean against them." Now the house was filled with men and women, and all the Philistine lords were there. On the roof were about three thousand men and women watching while Samson made sport. Samson called to the LORD, "O LORD God, remember me, I pray, and strengthen me just this time, O God, that I may avenge myself a vengeance from the Philistines for one of my two eyes." Then Samson grasped the two middle pillars upon which the house rested, and leaned upon them with his right hand and with his left hand. Samson said, "I shall die with the Philistines."[16] He bowed with his might and the house fell upon the lords and upon all the people who were in it. The dead that he slew at his death were many more than he had killed in his lifetime. His brothers and all his father's house went down, lifted him up, and went up, and buried him between Zorah and Eshtaol in the grave of Manoah his father. He had judged Israel twenty years.

[15]Read *ha'asirim.*
[16]Or jussive, "Let me die."

Introduction

The Samson narrative comprises four chapters in the Book of Judges, and consists of ninety-six verses. In the scope of this complex story, only three names occur: Manoah, Samson, and Delilah.[1] Since other significant characters in the story remain nameless, we may assume that these three names contribute something worthwhile to the overall message of the narrative. When we take account of the role played by names in the ancient world, and of the importance attributed to proper nomenclature, we learn to interpret certain signposts erected by narrators long ago. Such signs are often highly ambiguous; the reader must therefore constantly guard against misreading them.

Samson as a Solar Myth

Interpreters early seized the clue found within Samson's name, and carried it to extreme conclusions. Viewing the word Samson as a form of the root *šmš* (sun), critics understood the *on* ending as a diminutive. The result was "Little Sun." This identification of the hero with the sun suggested the possibility that a solar myth lay at the foundation of the story.[2] Certain features of the narrative gave considerable support to such an understanding of this strange account, and bits of evidence from other biblical texts seemed to remove all doubt about the theory's validity. References to Beth-shemesh and En-shemesh in the general vicinity within which the Samson story circulated pointed to a solar cult with its sacred temple and spring.

Evidence of a solar myth within the Samson narrative has been found in many of the episodes themselves. A Mithraic plaque[3] depicting a lion with a bee in its mouth raises the possibility that a solar myth about the proper month for locating honey (when the sun stands in the sign of Leo) lies behind the incident in which Samson slew a lion and subsequently found honey in its carcass. Similarly, certain rituals involving foxes existed in Roman solar worship. Ovid explained the ritual associated with the month Ceres as a result of a misfortune when a young boy captured a fox that had broken into a hen house, wrapped it in straw, and set it on fire, only to watch in horror as the fox escaped and ran through local grainfields.[4] In addition, partridges and asses were integral to solar worship in the ancient world, and stories exist of miraculous water sources provided by the sun god.

The seven locks of Samson's hair represented the sun's rays, and his blinding recalled the sun as a one-eyed God. Samson's death pointed to the similar fate of the sun, which pulls down the western pillars, upon which the heavenly vault stands, and brings darkness to all. Likewise, Samson's hiding in a rocky crag symbolized the sun's retreat behind dark clouds; just as Samson burst forth from hiding and destroyed his foes, so the sun's devastating power emerged from a violent storm. Furthermore, while Delilah's web pointed to winter's icy grip on the weakened sun, Samson's casting off the web and pin to free his hair pointed to the rays of the sun melting frozen nature. Delilah's name, connoting flirtation, suggested a relation to Ishtar, sacred to solar worship. Finally, a favorite epithet of the sun god Shamash, Judge, was said to be reflected in the clan name Dan, which comes from the root meaning "to judge."

In short, scholars searched far and wide to discover evidence that the Samson story was actually a solar myth. As usual in such endeavors, they overstated the case. As a result, few, if any, interpreters today accept the theory that Samson was a solar hero. Instead, they observe that ". . . the legend, which is very old, has its roots in the earth, not in the sky."[5] Such a view does not rule out the possibility that solar features occur in the Samson story, but it does minimize their significance.

Samson and Heracles

Striking similarities between Samson and Heracles have also given rise to much discussion.[6] Just as Heracles' wondrous feats were divided into twelve separate incidents, so Samson's exploits totaled an even dozen by some reckonings.[7] The similarities between the two are so compelling that arguments over originality surfaced: A Greek author claimed that the Greeks stole the story from the Hebrews,[8] and a Christian scholar has insisted that the two figures have little in common.[9]

Identical themes do suggest comparison of the two heroes. Both killed a lion with their bare hands, and both were betrayed by a woman. Each chose his death voluntarily, and did forced labor as a result of a weaker person's treachery. Both Samson and Heracles tore down gates or pillars, and each one groped around in darkness, Samson's a Philistine-made blindness, and Heracles' a journey in the Underworld.

Samson, the Natural Man

Sceptical of the solar theory, and dubious about the importance of affinities between Samson and Heracles, other scholars viewed the biblical hero as a child of nature.[10] Conflict between representatives of culture and of nature captured the imagination of the author who composed the Gilgamesh Epic. In this remarkable work Enkidu, a child of nature, surrendered to the charms of a harlot lass, who subsequently introduced him to a civilization over which Gilgamesh ruled. Although the two men fought one another at first, eventually they became fast friends. Perhaps Enkidu's early death signified the inability of natural man to survive under the changed circumstances brought about by his acculturation. Doubtless, the animals' rejection of Enkidu after his marathon cohabitation with a harlot implied that he could no longer remain a child of nature.[11]

In some ways, Samson fits the mold of a natural man quite snugly. He slew a lion without the aid of any weapon, and fought the Philistines with a crude weapon, the jawbone of an ass, which happened to be lying nearby.[12] When angry, he slipped away to a rocky crag, and to quench his thirst he drank water from a mortar. In addition, Samson scraped honey from the carcass of a lion, and, of course, let his hair flow freely. As a child of nature, he possessed remarkable strength, except in one area. His fatal flaw was a penchant for Philistine women: Without them he could not survive, and in their arms he courted disaster.[13]

His foes would naturally constitute cultural men and women. These Philistines dwelt in cities along fertile plains, and enjoyed the distinct advantages of cultivated fields. Danites, on the other hand, dwelt in the hills and paid homage to the powerful representatives of advanced culture. Whereas these rulers trimmed their hair, Samson allowed his locks to grow unchecked. Philistine women enhanced their appearance with expensive clothing, jewelry, and cosmetics, while their men wore the finest garments.[14]

This sharp contrast between Samson and his Philistine adversaries overlooked important facts. The story implies that such incidents as slaying a lion bare-handedly, eating honey taken from a lion's carcass, and drinking water from a mortar were highly unusual phenomena. In addition, Samson's flowing locks resulted from a Nazirite vow, while his use of an ass's jawbone was necessitated by the controlling aetiology associated with the story. Furthermore, Samson demonstrated remarkable wit in verbal exchange with the Philistines. Most importantly, Samson's ordinary domicile must have been no different from that of his enemies, except that it was on a higher elevation. In short, if Samson ever represented a child of nature struggling against cultural men (and women), the tale has carefully blurred all evidence for such an interpretation.

Thus far we have alluded to one name only, Samson. Two others occur in the Samson narrative and invite speculation. The name of Samson's father, Manoah, suggests rest,[15] while see p. 16 Delilah probably derives from a word meaning "affectionate."[16] In any event, both names clearly contain puns within context. The similarity between Delilah and the word for night *(layelah)* may partly explain the juxtaposition of the incident

at Gaza and the Delilah episode. In the space of three verses
(16:1–3), four occurrences of *layelah* stand out as noticeably as
the beautiful Timnite in her wedding festivities. Twice the
narrator tells us that the Gazites kept watch *all night,* and an
equal number of times he remarks that Samson lay until the
middle of the night, and got up in the middle of the night. The
name Delilah, then, made smooth transition between the two
unrelated episodes and continued the erotic mood introduced
by the earlier reference to a harlot.

Likewise the narrator may have chosen the name Manoah
because of its similarity to the word for cereal offering *(minchah)*. If this kinship is intentional, Manoah's addition of a
minchah to the burnt offering specified by the angel signified
Manoah's intellectual grasp of the clue provided him in regard
to the messenger's identity. Certainly the context emphasizes
the significance of a name, in this instance the identity of the
divine messenger, and suggests that disclosure takes place
without divulging full mystery.

The Samson Saga

In my view, the story of Samson belongs neither to solar
myth nor to nature legend, but comprises a saga.[17] As such it
makes use of mythical features and contains faint echos of the
conflict between the natural and the cultural. Saga, however,
takes minimal historical events and personages, and treats
them in elevated fashion. The events it proclaims, however,
stretch facticity to the breaking point. Saga abounds in exaggerated feats; it tends toward hyperbole, and treats the fantastic as if it were ordinary.

The Samson saga celebrates the miraculous birth of its
hero, traces his remarkable career in the arms of women and
in hand-to-hand combat with uncircumcised foes, describes his
reversal of fortune, and recounts his strange final act of
revenge that cost him dearly. It achieves sublimity in the wondrous story of the angel's disappearance, and approaches despair in depicting Samson's loss of the Lord and subsequent
ignominy. The saga extols Samson as mighty warrior and ad-

venturous lover, capable of wit in no small measure. Possessing a powerful sense of fair play, he wishes only to get revenge— and to be left alone. Accordingly, he allows no one to tell him what to do, whether it is his own father or his wife's. Still, the saga portrays its hero as a person who is subject to weakness, both with respect to Philistine women, and in regard to bodily needs. Lacking sufficient water to quench his thirst, this mighty Nazirite stared death in the face and acknowledged his dependence upon the Lord for survival. Again and again the saga focuses attention upon the ultimate source of Samson's strength. In this way the secular tone of the separate episodes becomes muted, and Samson succeeds in diverting attention from himself to the One who answered his prayer. In the end the child of promise lies in a borrowed grave, and leaves no sons or daughters to mourn his passing.

We cannot describe with any certainty the history of the composition of this notable saga. Presumably, certain solar features that characterized ancient Near Eastern religion, to-gether with reminiscences of conflict between children of na-ture and of culture, were common knowledge in Israel. An author, or several authors, combined these elements with a number of historical features: the Philistines who resided in the cities of Gaza, Askelon, and the valley of Soreq; Danites, who lived in the hill country of Mahaneh-dan, Hebron, Zorah, Eshtaol; men of Judah; place names, like Ramath-lehi and En Haqqore. To these he or she added folkloric motifs: the three riddles; the episode of the foxes; the slaying of a lion and discov-ery of honey in its carcass. In addition, the author made gener-ous use of familiar motifs and themes found throughout Israel's literary corpus. These traditions include, among others: (1) the barren wife; (2) the helpless hero before a woman's wiles; (3) the quest for the divine name; (4) the death wish; (5) the loss of charisma; and (6) terror over theophany. The author also used, or composed, riddles, aetiologies, prayers, victory songs, a birth announcement, and a recognition story.

This diverse material achieved a degree of coherence when woven into the fabric of Samson's heroic exploits. Legendary accretions gave the story additional power, and tragic religious

elements increased the saga's pathos. The author made full use
of rich rhetorical devices inherent within the Hebrew language, polishing the prose to make it suitable for epic themes.
Here and there was sprinkled a poetic text or two, sometimes
a rare one replete with a repetitious final sound.

In time the Deuteronomistic editor seems to have inserted
certain framing statements; by this means Samson became a
judge in a long line of distinguished deliverers of Israel, and his
life was subsumed under a grandiose theory of divine action in
Israel's historical existence.[18] Certain explanatory glosses also
arose, reminding later Israelites that Philistines had once
ruled their ancestors, and remarking that bridegrooms used to
give seven-day drinking feasts in Israel.

Aesthetic Criticism

The Samson saga has captured the imagination of countless
interpreters.[19] Biblical critics have approached the text from
nearly every conceivable perspective, while artists, poets, and
dramatists have given their understanding of the story for
countless viewers and listeners.[20] Surely we risk overinterpret-
ing the saga. What possible reason exists for offering yet another analysis of the familiar story?

I have two responses to this question, although granting its
peculiar force. First, every generation must wrestle with
ancient texts, testing their message in the light of new experiences and understandings of reality. The task of biblical interpretation never ends: Upon each new generation, ancient texts
lay special claims which ought not to be taken at face value, but
to be justified anew. Second, insofar as I know, no one has
analyzed the Samson saga in precisely the way I wish to do. I
call my approach aesthetic criticism, by which I mean sensitivity to the beauty and art of a literary piece.[21]

I shall permit the method to speak for itself. I do wish,
however, to make five observations that may not be self-
evident.

Suspension of Disbelief

Aesthetic criticism endeavors to accept the narrative at face
value, and seeks to delineate the ramifications of the story as

fully as possible. It enters into the spirit of the text being
studied insofar as possible, rather than quarreling about the
absurdity or illogicality of any given incident or statement. The
aesthetic critic tries to view the story from the perspective of
the author or narrator. He, or she, *believes* the story, or rather,
believes the story *as story*. This means that the critic writes as
if all things are possible, as indeed they are in saga. Readers
should be forewarned, then, that such a stance does not imply
acceptance on the factual level at all. For example, although I
regard the Samson story as almost entirely lacking in historical basis, I shall discuss the saga as if it actually transpired. In
one sense it has taken place—in the minds of the author and
untold numbers of persons who have heard or read the narrative.

The Intentional Fallacy

Although one can never be absolutely certain that he or she
has captured the real intention of the author,[22] in my view the
text offers decisive clues that enable the critic to expound the
rich meanings of separate incidents and of the larger unit with
confidence that (s)he has not completely distorted the author's
purpose or purposes. These important signposts function as
rhetorical devices of all kinds; study of these narrative aids is
still in its infancy.[23] We shall, therefore, stumble in semi-dark-
ness like Samson in Gazite captivity; but we hope to r take some
progress in the process.

The Lost World

At the same time that we have lost full access to the mind
of the author, we have also been deprived of numerous givens
that greeted any story in the ancient world.[24] The author could
presuppose certain kinds of information and familiarity with
various motifs that we perceive only dimly. Key words, phrases,
sounds, and symbols evoked a whole world for the ancient Israelite that remains largely hidden from our view. Gestures, too,
and intonations enabled narrators to enrich a story in a manner that is lost forever. One way we can compensate for this
grievous loss is through imaginative reconstruction. Accord-

ingly, the aesthetic critic travels first one path and then another, in the same manner in which Søren Kierkegaard explicated the story of the sacrifice of Isaac.[25] By this means the critic hopes to recreate part of that lost world.

Juxtaposition

Certain themes recur regularly in ancient literature. Because of their frequent occurrence, authors customarily built upon fully developed traditions, altering them to fit new understandings of reality. As a result of this practice, the critic needs to study motifs in widely disparate texts, paying attention to the possibility that one account may illuminate another at crucial junctures. Juxtaposition of related texts provides an important perspective from which to understand the special viewpoint of each author who dealt with a particular motif. The aesthetic critic seeks to relate similar themes from the entire Hebrew corpus, and beyond. Juxtaposition also applies within a single text. Close scrutiny of the sequence of words, ideas, or moods in a literary unit often corrects a first impression that the material has been brought together haphazardly. In short, the critic needs to cultivate the practice of associative thinking, so that certain signals immediately lead to fresh discovery.

Continuity

The task of all interpretation is to bridge the chasm between two worlds, those of the story and of the contemporary reader. The first and third observations above emphasize the gulf between the world view of the saga[26] and that of present day appropriators of the biblical heritage, while the second and fourth suggest ways the text itself brings the two worlds together. All four contain clues to assist the critic in the task of understanding. They presuppose a fifth, namely, continuity at the deeper levels of existence between ancient peoples and their modern counterparts. Certain human concerns transcend temporal and spatial boundaries.[27] The aesthetic critic searches for such links connecting then and now, there and here. He or she avoids psychologization of a text while remaining alert to powerful character portrayal. Indeed, the critic shrinks from neither the ecstasy nor the pathos of a story, but allows both to evoke feelings of awe and dread.

This book explores the search for the unknown in the context of desire to retain mystery. Tension mounts as various individuals press for full information, while others press precious data to their bosoms. Excitement surges as those seeking knowledge taste the sweetness of success, and sorrow abounds when others fail to conceal vital secrets. If the ancient biblical proverb approaches the truth that God's glory consists in concealing mystery while a king's crowning achievement is in searching things out (Proverbs 25:2), then the heroes and heroines within the Samson saga deserve thrones and kingdoms. Each searched, by whatever means necessary, until the quest ended triumphantly.

In the Samson narrative, four dark secrets yielded to persistent inquiry, or rather, three succumbed to active search and a fourth simply gave itself up without the slightest resistance. Reluctantly, the heavenly messenger supplied Manoah a decisive clue to his identity that enabled Samson's father to recognize that he was standing in the presence of the Lord. Besieged by his wife's ceaseless tears during their wedding celebration, an unhappy Samson divulged the true meaning of his riddle that had baffled the thirty Philistines. Similarly, the unfortunate Nazirite opened his heart to a talkative lover because he could endure her verbal assaults no longer. In each case the interplay between concealment and quest for information fills the episode to the breaking point. Twice the possessor of new knowledge promptly passed it on to interested persons; only Manoah harbored his newfound treasure from others. We have spoken thus far of three secrets; a fourth lingers in the background of the story. While Samson cavorted with a harlot at Gaza, his enemies surrounded the house and concealed their intention to ambush the Danite. Samson's premature departure with an unusual burden implies that he became aware of their nefarious plan without initiating the slightest search.

In all four episodes discovery came at another's expense; shared information cost dearly. In the case of the angel, who surrendered his special name as a wonder-working deity, the new relationship brought an end to earthly communion. Never again did the heavenly envoy appear to Manoah and his perceptive wife. The carefully laid plans of ambush in Gaza became wasted effort once a satiated lover discovered villainy crouching in the dark. But when Samson gave up vital information instead of receiving it, he suffered the consequences of folly. The first forfeiture cost Samson wedded bliss with the Timnite who was the right one in his eyes. The second disclosure precipitated his loss of sight, freedom, and life.

Surprisingly, no one uttered an ecstatic shout upon arriving at the end of a successful search for hidden mystery. Bent upon exposing his enemies to attack from without, Samson removed the gates of the city to a distant hill, defying the Gazites to retrieve their protective door. The Timnite heaved a sigh of relief, confident that she had rescued herself from a fiery death, and Delilah excitedly awaited payment in silver for her treachery. Only Manoah, joined by his unnamed wife, caught a glimpse of the danger of treading too deeply in forbidden territory.

Dubious motives accompanied the active quest for knowledge belonging to another. At the very best, Manoah's persistence before an angel's reticence sprang from an unwillingness to accept mystery as a necessary ingredient of human discourse. His attempt to excuse his probing by resorting to the messenger's vanity scarcely justified the bold inquiry. Perhaps his stammering syntax communicates his own uneasiness over the situation. The thirty guests at Samson's wedding pressed for secret information with one goal in mind: to win their wager with Samson at any cost. Delilah, too, sought monetary gain for her dangerous pursuit of knowledge from the mighty Samson whose strength was no match for her charms.

Questionable means for achieving precious data found expression in two instances, and perhaps in a third. Fearing that they would lose their bet with Samson and suffer the accompanying loss of face, the thirty Philistines threatened to burn Samson's fiancee along with her father's house. Desperate from this terrible threat, the Timnite resorted to copious tears by night. Delilah's cohorts relied upon their wealth to persuade her, and she concocted a game of tease that set the stage for a considerably more powerful weapon, verbal abuse. Perhaps, too, Manoah's resort to prayer and flattery came perilously close to manipulating the emissary from heaven.

For years I have studied this thrilling account of concealment and search, hoping to catch a fleeting glimpse of hidden treasure but wary lest I fail to perceive its sanctity. The story has willingly yielded some secrets, grudgingly others, and has resolutely refused to divulge still others. If I finally set this book free—and thus declare for one and all what has become precious to me—I trust it will enable some readers to grasp the meaning of the saga more fully.

Chapter One
Literary and Stylistic Traditions

A Dying Man's Legacy

Dying words linger in our memory long after other pronouncements have fallen victim to the oblivion of past time. So significant were deathbed utterances that a literary form evolved early in ancient Israel governing the character of testaments.[1] A patriarch's final wishes established destinies. His sons and grandsons waited anxiously for the paternal blessing, and implemented it by word and deed. The occasion of the dying word was solemn, one could even say sacred. For it was then that a father voiced his most precious wish for his children, and at this time that his priorities captured the imaginations of all involved.

The patriarch Abraham's fundamental concern for his son's wellbeing evoked a solemn oath from Eliezer, the old faithful servant, that he would secure a wife for Isaac from Abraham's relatives, and that, failing in this venture, he would not permit Isaac to return to Mesopotamia (Genesis 24:1–9). Abraham's sole concern was that Isaac avoid connubial alliances with the daughters of Canaanites. Experience had taught him that the God of heaven and earth would see to his promise articulated at Abraham's call and reiterated at decisive stages in the patriarch's pilgrimage.

Although the text lacks clarity, it may imply that returning to Mesopotamia was even worse than intermarriage with the local Canaanites. In any case, Abraham conceded that Eliezer would be free from his oath if the woman refused to accompany him to the land of promise. He did not, however, budge an inch on the matter of giving up access to the land to which God had brought him. Perhaps the brief stay in Egypt had taught Abraham the futility of resorting to his own expediency for salvation. Better still, perhaps he had slowly perceived the significance of the land in God's plan for him and his descendants.[2] At the most, this hallowed land had become the locus of all that he treasured. Here he had stumbled from revelation to revelation, from self-discovery to utter reliance upon the divine promise. Isaac, too, must walk this road of faith.

Last words could cause consternation as well as great rejoicing. This unforgettable message arises from Isaac's final blessing[3] of his sons. Utter deceit elicited a blessing for the unintended son Jacob, and sped him on a journey that increased the possibility of his marrying a Hittite. Alarmed by the repercussions of her scheme to obtain a blessing for her favorite son, Jacob's mother confessed that life to her would lose its meaning if he chose a wife from the daughters of the Hittites (Genesis 27:46). Esau, too, experienced a lion's share of grief as a result of his father's misdirected blessing. The feeble substitute for a blessing hardly eased the pain, inasmuch as he was destined to serve his younger brother. Esau's reaction to his mother's anxiety about marriage to Canaanites, though entirely proper, only highlights his bitter plight. To please his father, so he thought, Esau took additional wives from Ishmael.

Jacob's final blessing for his *grandsons* gave affront to Joseph who had sustained his father during the great famine (Genesis 48:17–19). Despite Joseph's protest, his aged father exercised an independent spirit by crossing his arms and placing his right hand upon Ephraim, the youngest son.

The last words of Jacob in regard to his twelve sons give voice to a combination of recorded memory and anticipated destiny. Similarly, Moses praised the Lord and pronounced blessings upon the several tribes of Israel that had acknowledged his leadership. The mighty King David used the occasion of the deathbed scene to tie up all loose ends in his political fortune (1 Kings 2:1–9). These instructions, cruel in the extreme, enabled David to die in peace, and established the kingdom under Solomon.

"Testaments" such as these reveal more about Israel's cherished memories and values than they record actual events, with the possible exception of King David. They tell us what concerns motivated the lives of those who shaped the literary traditions in ancient Israel.[4] These men and women who fashioned the individual and collective memory into poetic units and narrative strands recognized the power generated by final words and used this literary device generously.

In Israel, as elsewhere, some dying words retain their power even when not associated with deathbed blessings. Who can forget the mortally wounded Saul's desperate plea to his armorbearer: "Draw your sword and thrust me through with it, lest these uncircumcised come and thrust me through, and make sport of me"? The deep tragedy of Israel's first king's life dogged him to his dying moment. Even his faithful armorbearer, fearful of touching God's anointed whom even David had dared not kill, refused to obey the king's command. In desperation Saul fell upon his own sword. But the scene does not end here. He who had refused his master's dying request demonstrated his loyalty by falling upon his own sword and dying with King Saul (1 Samuel 31:1–6).

Saul's final cry echoed that of another great antagonist of the Philistines. Humiliated by his uncircumcised captors, and groping blindly in artificial darkness, Samson breathed his last gasp with a prayer on his oft-kissed lips. In those four Hebrew words rests the real tragedy of Samson: "Let me die with the Philistines" (Judges 16:30a). Having made his bed with their daughters, he now chose to die in concert with the uncircumcised.[5] Samson could not separate himself from the Philistines in life or in death. This was Samson's personal dilemma, and it governed his every action. Alienated from his own people, he entrusted himself to the arms and hearts of those who held him in dread contempt. In the end, they did him in, and he gladly reciprocated.

Perchance his final sigh belongs to a category other than prayer. In that case, Samson died with a word of resignation: "I shall die with the Philistines." If this translation is allowed, it suggests that Samson saw grim humor in his tragic end. With the barest hint of a chuckle on his lips and the slightest grin on his countenance, Samson fell into the hands of the God who fashioned Philistine and Israelite. Regardless of whether we understand Samson's dying words as resignation or prayer, they occurred in a prayer context. For him and for the era, such piety was highly unusual. Twice the traditions about Samson preserved a prayer on the lips of one who devoted most of his time to harlots and coquettes, or to slaying the enemy. Such unexpected petitions from Israel's strongest hero merit close scrutiny, precisely because they admit that even one who scoffed at convention, laughed at danger, and courted ruin did not escape the necessity of prayer.[6]

Literary Forms

Prayers

The first prayer we shall consider occurs in connection with Samson's slaughter of one thousand Philistines with a wholly unconventional weapon, the jawbone of an ass. Thoroughly exhausted from his military exploit—or was it from wracking his brain to come up with an appropriate battle cry?—Samson experienced great thirst. Confronted by his mortality, he sought assistance from one stronger than he. Calling upon the Lord, he said

> Thou hast given into the hand of thy servant this great deliverance, and now I am about to die with thirst, and I shall fall into the hand of the uncircumcised (Judges 15:18).*

The Lord whose angel had announced the birth of this thirsty warrior, and who had used him to afflict the Philistines, acted decisively to rescue his servant. He brought forth water at Lehi, and revived Samson.

Several literary features of this prayer and its immediate context call for comment, particularly since they signify the great care with which this brief unit was crafted. We begin with a word play, a favorite device in Israelite literature.[7] In this

---

*Unless otherwise stated, all translations are the author's.

case it may be accidental, but the similarity both in sound and in radicals between *matsa'* and *tsama'* warns us to pay close attention to the vocabulary employed. The author could easily have chosen another word than *wayyimtsa'* (and he found); instead, she or he transposed the first two letters and described Samson's thirst *(wayyitsma'* and *batstsama')*. Even the adverb qualifying this thirst contains as its first two letters the final letters of the previous word *(wayyitsma' me'od)*. Two other similarities in sound occur, the personal pronoun *'attah* (Thou) and temporal adverb *'attah* (now). The former reflects unaccustomed familiarity, the latter Samson's impatience that surfaces elsewhere in the saga (14:2).

We note that Samson merely cried out to the Lord. Shunning ritual or special vocabulary of entreaty, he simply spoke to the Lord confident that he would be heard. In this instance the author used the Tetragrammaton, the sacred name YHWH,[8] although he or she shifted to the more general word for God in describing the divine response. That Samson prayed gives cause for astonishment. That he identified himself as the Lord's servant boggles the imagination. Nothing in the saga prepares the way for or justifies in the slightest this self-designation. Had he called himself a Nazirite,[9] the birth story would have provided grounds for such a claim, and the final episode would have confirmed its appropriateness for the narrative at one level. But "thy servant" fits Samson's lips as poorly as prayer itself.

The great deliverance that Samson mentioned as God's gift failed to take into account Samson's expenditure of energy, unless that is the force of the reference to his hand. Be that as it may, the language derives from Israel's tradition of decisive victories wrought by divine presence and power, deliverance celebrated in names like Joshua.[10] The narrator juxtaposes victory at the hand of Samson and the threat of defeat into the hand of the uncircumcised. The word choice here misses the opportunity of a clever pun, that between *wenapalti* (and I shall fall) and *pilishtim* (Philistines). For that reason we ought to pause at this word of opprobrium, the uncircumcised. Precisely in this characteristic of the Hebrews, highly rare in the ancient world, lay a distinctive theological issue. The Philistines did not belong to the covenant people, for they did not wear the sign of allegiance on their bodies.

In his worry over falling into the hands of the uncircumcised, Samson joins hands with King Saul, who feared lest the uncircumcised come and thrust him through and make sport[11] of him. In this respect Samson was less fortunate, from our point of view, than Saul, whose corpse became the object of derision. The uncircumcised got their hands on Samson's body while he was very much alive, and they made sport as he groped around in his Philistine-made darkness. Nay, they created his darkness, and precipitated his suicide, just as their descendants brought about Saul's self-destruction.

What did Samson dread? Was it Saul's anxiety lest his mortally wounded body become subject to torture? Or was it dread of his corpse falling into unfriendly hands, as happened to Saul? Perhaps the narrator intended both meanings. One thing appears certain—the phrase "and I shall fall into the hand of the uncircumcised," anticipates Samson's destiny. By this means the narrator points forward to the actual fall into hostile hands and ultimately to the collapse of an edifice built and peopled by these uncircumcised foes.

The story anticipates subsequent narration in yet another regard. As a consequence of drinking from the marvelous source, Samson regains his strength and comes alive ("He drank, his spirit returned, and he revived"). Two things stand out in this observation: the use of spirit rather than strength, and the word for coming alive. While spirit *(ruach)* can mean stamina, it more properly refers to psychic wellbeing.[12] The ambiguity may even be purposive: Samson had come perilously near death, and regained his life by drinking from God-given water. The word "he came alive" *(wayyechi)* gives the appearance of redundancy until one follows the narrative to its denouement. In that final episode the antithesis to this notion of revivification punctuates the text. There Samson fell into the hands of the Philistines and *died.* Lest we fail to see the connection between the two texts, the narrator erected a sign in full view. This word, *life,* is repeated in the midst of a concatenation of usages of the word for death.

> The *dead* that he *slew* at his *death* were more than he *killed* in his *lifetime* (16:30b).

Another prayer within the Samson narrative makes possible this slaughter of the enemy. It, too, uses ordinary language and shuns ritual. Actually, the identical formula introduces both prayers, except that one specifies Samson whereas the other uses the personal pronoun. This formula, "and Samson called upon the Lord and said," belongs to normal usage of early biblical tradition. Samson's threefold appeal to God strikes one as strange, but underlines the intensity of the request.

> Now Samson called upon the *Lord* and said, "O *Lord Yahweh,* remember me, I pray, and strengthen me, I pray, just this once, O *God,* that I may get revenge from the Philistines—a vengeance for one of my two eyes."

The appeal for remembrance functions to underscore Samson's great sense of abandonment, for had he not betrayed the sacred trust? In most eyes his sorry plight only confirmed the suspicion of God-forsakenness; having run roughshod over the divine vocation, Samson reaped the consequences of his behavior. Grinding at the Philistines' mill had given him ample time to imagine that God had forgotten him. In light of his reprehensible track record, how could it be otherwise? Therefore, Samson begged to be remembered again—after all, he had given God some pleasant moments—in the hope that he would be moved to compassion. That faint hope led Samson to make another bold request. He asked nothing less than restoration of his remarkable strength. But he knew that even that much was pressing his luck; consequently, he added a qualification "just this time." Surprisingly, he did not beg for renewed sight—or, indeed for a great deliverance so that he could thereafter demonstrate his loyalty and gratitude.

Twice a particle of entreaty occurs in this prayer. It follows each of the two requests for remembrance and renewed strength. In the other prayer Samson never resorted to such entreaty. In fact, in it he made no explicit request. Instead, his appeal remained completely implicit. That prayer contained praise and implied defeat of the supplicant. Conceivably, we should translate "and shall . . . I fall into the hand of the uncircumcised?" (RSV) This interpretation brings into the open the half-concealed request. Still, the alternative translation, "and I shall fall into the hand of the uncircumcised," makes supplication in its own way. The second prayer, on the other hand, gives no pretense about its intention. Samson's sorry state did not lend itself to praise. His memory of great deliverances dimmed by the ceaseless grinding at the enemy mill, and his victory song drowned out by the din of a counter-song and the laughter of sport at his expense, Samson came directly to the point. *"Please* remember me and strengthen me."

In neither prayer context did God answer verbally. Instead, he responded by providing precisely what Samson needed or requested. Nevertheless, the Jewish commentator Gersonides has appropriately honored Samson in the following way: "When he called upon the Lord he was answered." (Commentary to 1 Samuel 12:11)[13]

The Samson saga records still another prayer, this one from the hero's father. Stunned by the good news brought to him by a barren wife upon whom God had bestowed renewed hope, Manoah begged the Lord to send the messenger again so he could obtain further information about the promised son.

> Now Manoah entreated the Lord, "Pray let the man of God whom you sent come again to us, O Lord, and teach us what we shall do for the lad who will be born" (13:8).

The forcefulness of the request touched a responsive chord, and God heeded Manoah's words. Still, he answered the prayer in his own way. Manoah asked that the man of God appear again to *them.* Instead, he came to the wife a second time. Through her initiative, Manoah obtained an opportunity to question the man of God, whose sharp retort only repeated the original instructions, and warned Manoah to see that they were carried out fully.

Here we note entirely different vocabulary for prayer from that used by Samson. Instead of calling God *(qara')*,[14] Manoah makes supplication by means of cultic language. Originally the term *'atar* signified an incense offering.[15] Later it came to connote the prayer itself rather than the ritual connected with a fervent request. Manoah addressed his prayer to "the Lord": The response came from God, although strong textual evidence favors restoration of the personal name for Israel's God.[16] Confusion may have developed from the twofold reference to the man of *God* and angel of *God*. In any event, Manoah demonstrated profound faith in a promise transmitted to him secondhand. The prayer takes for granted the reliability of the announced birth. Such good news possessed inherent plausibility, originating as it did in God's own messenger. Manoah simply believed what his wife told him, and hungered for additional information. Thus he turned to the Lord in prayer.

Before leaving the prayers within the Samson narrative, let us note that they cannot be separated from the larger context. Each presupposes events recorded in the saga. Samson's first prayer alludes to "this great deliverance," specifically his slaughter of one thousand Philistines with the jawbone of an ass. We have already seen, too, that the prayer offers a word play on "and he found" from the narrative recounting this episode. Samson's final prayer likewise presupposes the story, particularly in the reference to vengeance for one of his two eyes. Manoah's prayer, too, grows out of the larger story and can only be understood in light of the narrative of Samson's birth.

Aetiologies

Samson's first prayer is embedded within a context that has two topographical aetiologies.[17] One aetiology explains the origin of the "Hill of the Jawbone"; the other identifies the situation that gave rise to the naming of "Partridge Spring." To commemorate his marvelous victory over a thousand Philistines with no weapon but an ass's jawbone, Samson names the site of the battle "Hill of the Jawbone." In all probability certain physical features of the hill in question resembled the jawbone of an ass. The tradition about Samson's use of this piece of an ass's anatomy in hand to hand combat naturally led to incorporation of an aetiology of Ramath-Lehi into the Samson saga.

The other aetiology connects with the Samson narrative in a much more subtle fashion. It picks up the word for Samson's entreaty and combines it with spring, arriving at "Spring of the One Who Called." Now another meaning of the caller is partridge, in all likelihood, the original sense of *haqqore'* here. If so, the association with Samson's prayer for water has supplanted an earlier occasion that gave rise to the name, "Partridge Spring." Of the two, only this aetiology has the customary formula: "Therefore its name was called . . . which is at . . . until this day."[18]

Victory Songs

Two victory songs embellish the Samson saga. The first occurs in connection with the slaughter of the Philistines at the Hill of the Jawbone.

> With the jawbone of the ass, ass upon asses, with the jawbone of the ass I have slain a thousand men (15:16).[19]

In this brief song of nine words, ass occurs four times, jawbone twice. Three words alone proclaim the heroic act: "I have slain a thousand men." Unlike Moses and Miriam, who *sang (shir, 'anan)* their triumphant song after the miracle at the Reed Sea (Exodus 15:1,21), Samson *says* his little ditty.

The Philistines' victory celebration exceeds Samson's in repetition of a single sound.

> *Our* god has given into *our* hands Samson *our* enemy. . . . *Our* god has given *our* enemy into *our* hands, and the ravager of *our* land, who has killed many *of us* (16:23b, 24b).

Eight times the first person plural ending *enu* punctuates the joyous shout. As in the case of Samson's song, we cannot reproduce in English the precise effect of the Hebrew text.

Theologically, the two songs stand worlds apart. Samson's breathes the spirit of braggadocio; the Philistines praise their god. Samson could not bring himself to share the glory which he alone had made possible. No reflection upon the coincidence of a handy weapon or his unusual stamina led Samson to acknowledge a little help from his God. The Philistines, on the other hand, lauded their god for delivering Samson into their hands, when from our perspective they had secured him through bribery and deceit. Of course we must not ignore the occasion for their rejoicing—a great sacrifice to Dagon. Their language reflects the cultic reality of a solemn assembly. Samson attended no such sacred gathering and felt no compunction to praise God for his own mighty feat.

Riddles

A different act of courage gave birth to one of two (three?) riddles that enliven the Samson story.[20] The bare-handed victory over a roaring lion and subsequent discovery of honey in its carcass enabled Samson to pose an insoluble riddle to the thirty Philistines attending his wedding celebration.

> Food came from the eater; sweetness came from strength (14:14a).

The Philistines framed their answer, grudgingly given them by Samson's endangered spouse, with a comparable riddle.

> What is sweeter than honey, and what is stronger than a lion (14:18a)?

Not to be outdone, Samson responded with yet another riddle-like retort.

> Had you not plowed with my heifer, you would not have found out my riddle (14:18b).

We shall examine these riddles in greater detail later. For the moment it suffices to observe that the Samson narrative utilizes two riddles and one riddle-like saying in an effort to demonstrate Samson's sole right to claim the title "lion of the village."[21]

Heroic Exploits

Neither the fervent prayers, nor the joyous victory songs, nor even the riddles justify Samson's claim to fame. That renown rests on his mighty exploits at the expense of the Philistines. Although some interpreters have attempted to discover twelve heroic feats and thus to view Samson as an Israelite Hercules, we shall mention only five such demonstrations of remarkable strength.

The first grew out of Samson's riddle contest and precipitated two additional encounters with hostile Philistines. Thirty companions who attended Samson's wedding obtained vital information by threatening to burn his wife and her father if she did not tell them the secret to Samson's riddle. Successful in solving the enigma, the thirty men demanded the agreed-upon garments from Samson. In hot anger Samson journeyed to Askelon and slew thirty inhabitants, taking from their corpses the necessary items of clothing. These he handed over to the wedding guests who had won the wager and humiliated Samson.

Anger prompted Samson to return to his parents without the newly acquired bride, who was quickly given to Samson's best man.[22] Some time later he returned to Timnah to visit his wife, only to learn that her father had given her to another man. Again Samson sought revenge for wrongs directed at his person. Having caught three hundred foxes, he tied them by their tails and set torches between them. Then he turned them loose in grain fields and olive orchards to wreak havoc upon the Philistine food supply. Those who had lost their food stuffs quickly discovered Samson's hiding place and marched against the territory of Judah. Only too glad to save their necks, these people of Judah turned a securely bound Samson over to the Philistines. But the spirit of the Lord came mightily upon Samson, who threw off the ropes, seized a jawbone of an ass, and slew a thousand men.

The fourth heroic deed came in connection with Samson's visit to a harlot at Gaza. With Gazites lying in wait to capture him at daybreak, Samson arose in the middle of the night and walked away unscathed. On his shoulders he carried away the bronze door of the city gate, and the two posts that held it in place. Samson did not discard this heavy burden until he reached the top of a faraway hill in front of Hebron.[23]

The fifth episode spelled the end for Samson and his foes. Blinded, enslaved, mocked by his captors, Samson brought down the entire house of the Philistines upon those strong shoulders that had earlier transported Gaza's gates to a distant hill. This time the burden was overwhelming, and Samson perished with the uncircumcised throng in the doomed house.

Two of these five exploits are attributed to the power of the Spirit, which came mightly upon Samson at the moment of the feat. The mischief-making with foxes and the parade from Gaza's gates, on the other hand, are not associated with seizure by the Spirit of the Lord. The final episode does not mention the Spirit, but Samson's prayer implies an external source for his resurgent strength. In short, only two of five heroic deeds accord with the interpretation of Samson as a Nazirite, one whose strength is a permanent possession deriving in some mysterious way from an earlier vow.

Birth Story

This view of Samson as a Nazirite from birth derives from the story of his wondrous birth.[24] An angel appeared to Manoah's barren wife and announced the birth of a son. The mother-to-be must observe the laws of the Nazirite and see that her son does the same. Manoah prayed that the messenger return, and sought further information from him. The angel would only repeat his earlier message. The boy was born, and received the name "Samson."

Recognition Story

A recognition story stands alongside the birth narrative. The woman's intuitive identification of the man of God as one whose countenance resembled the angel of God is confirmed in holy fire. Having prevailed upon the man of God to tarry long enough for him to prepare a sacrifice, and having obtained a hint as to the angel's true identity, Manoah offered a burnt offering and a cereal offering upon a rock to him who performs wonders. The angel rose to heaven in the flame, and Manoah feared death until his wife assured him that God meant no harm to either of them.

Such are the traditions making up the Samson saga: prayers, victory songs, aetiologies, riddles, heroic deeds, birth story, and recognition story. The Samson narrative itself consists of four episodes: (1) a birth story and a recognition scene; (2) a marriage to a Timnite woman; (3) a visit to a harlot at Gaza; and (4) the Delilah incident and its sequel. For the moment we shall withhold comment about these four episodes.

Editorial Additions to the Saga

We turn rather to consider evidence that these individual stories were edited during a period subsequent to the events they record. The initial verse of the saga gives voice to a view that scholars have labeled Deuteronomistic.[25] According to this interpretation of Israel's history, virtue prospers a nation and vice leads to oppression from without. Thus we read that the Israelites continued to do evil in the Lord's eyes, and he gave them into the hand of Philistines forty years (13:1). Elsewhere Samson's tenure as judge is said to have lasted twenty years (15:20; 16:31). How can one explain the discrepancy of twenty years? Now Samson was not the last judge of Israel, although none follows him in the book by that title. Instead, two entirely unrelated episodes now separate the Samson saga from the stories of the last great judge, Samuel. He, too, judged Israel for twenty years during Philistine oppression. The judgeships of Samson and Samuel add up to forty years, most likely the forty years of Philistine rule alluded to in 13:1.[26] If so, we have evidence that an editor fit the Samson narrative into a much more comprehensive account of Israel's early history.

Redactional activity also produced an obscure reference to an exploit of the youthful Samson that has fallen out of the text. We have only the slightest hint that Yahweh's spirit began to stir Samson at Mahaneh-dan, between Zorah and Eshtaol (13:25). Unfortunately, we have no further information about the manner in which Samson displayed divine stirring. Only the general location of this virgin activity survived. Ironically, it became the scene of his final resting place.

Two additional remarks call for comment. In connection with the marriage preparations recorded in chapter 14, it is stated that the Lord was seeking an occasion against the Philistines.[27] The editor hastened to add that "at that time the Philistines were ruling over Israel" (14:4b).[28] Evidently time had been kind to Israelites, so much so that Philistine rule over them had nearly faded from memory. Hence an editor felt the need to explain that Philistines had ruled over Israel at one time. Similarly, Samson's wedding festivities at Timnah must have struck readers unfamiliar with *tsadiqah* marriage[29] as strange. "Why did the seven day feast take place at the bride's home?" they must have asked. To explain this unusual custom, an editor wrote a brief comment that such a procedure was at that time entirely proper, "for so young men used to do" (14:10b).

Twice we encounter an editorial summing up of Samson's activity. How can we explain two summary observations when one suffices? We expect a remark to the effect that he judged Israel twenty years at the end of the story. Does its recurrence suggest that the Samson saga once ended at 15:20 and that the Delilah episode was added subsequently?[30] Hardly. In my view, the aetiology of "Partridge Spring" belonged to a separate strand of tradition and was affixed to the Samson saga because of the identity of that spring at Lehi. To facilitate this association with the Samson saga, an editor added a comment about his judging Israel for twenty years. In short, the extra summary legitimates an aetiology. It does not follow that the Delilah episode was lacking in an earlier account. Instead, the brief aetiology of "Partridge Spring" did not belong to the earliest Samson saga.

Motifs

The Samson narrative is particularly rich in folklore motifs. In this connection, we wish to discuss six motifs: the barren wife; the hero helpless before a woman's wiles; the quest for a deity's name; the death wish of a hero; the loss of charisma; and the terror over theophany.

The Barren Wife

The motif of a barren wife[31] supplied a basic fund for early Israelite narratives. It arose in a culture that placed a premium on childbearing, one that even devised means of assuring progeny to a man who died without children.[32] In Israel and also in surrounding cultures a barren wife was known to resort to extreme measures to obtain children for her husband, even by substituting a slave for herself. A barren widow could practice harlotry in certain circumstances (Genesis 38) without censure; a wife could also make use of mandrakes and other objects to encourage pregnancy. In view of the stigma of childlessness, one had to take extreme measures to secure a child.

The patriarchal narratives make much of the barren woman. This motif pervades the story of Abraham, who had to wait patiently for a son as his barren wife passed the stage of bearing, and who finally held the son of promise in his arms as a sacrificial victim. Abraham's acquiescence in Sarah's gift of Hagar as a substitute wife only heightened the suspense generated by Sarah's closed womb. Similarly, Rachel endured the humiliation of childlessness while her rival bore children with reckless abandon. Her desperate plea, "Give me children, or I shall die!" (Genesis 30:1) and her willingness to purchase mandrakes to induce pregnancy by sharing her husband with Leah for a night of pleasure demonstrate the heavy burden childlessness brought.

Hannah's great distress of spirit robbed her of the ability to speak in God's presence. Instead of voicing her anxiety, she prayed in her heart. Sorely vexed year after year by a rival wife who had many children, and hardly consoled by knowledge of her husband's love, she asked the Lord for a son and then promised that son back in gratitude. The Lord heard her prayer and communicated his favor through Eli the priest of Shiloh (1 Samuel 1:1–20).

Certain elements characterize all of these stories. While each account has its special traits, and one should not force the material into a single mold, five things stand out above all else: (1) a preferred wife is barren; (2) another wife mocks her; (3) she begs for progeny; (4) a son is promised; (5) the son is born. Variations occur according to differing situations in narrative art. The Samson saga transforms the motif inasmuch as it discards the notion of a rival wife. On the other hand, it restores the idea of a heavenly visitor who announces the coming of a son (cf. Genesis 18), which is missing in the stories of Rachel and Hannah. Astonishingly, no special request for a child appears in the Samson saga.

The masculine references in this discussion require a word of explanation. In none of these stories does the fortunate wife give birth to a daughter. This fact alone points to an ethos far different from ours.[33] Although the stories never really articulate it, they surely imply that only the birth of a son completely removes the curse of barrenness. One travels a smooth road from these stories to Sirach's familiar observation that the birth of a son brings rejoicing but that of a daughter elicits sadness.[34]

A Hero Helpless Before a Woman's Wiles

The second motif to claim our attention is that of a hero helpless before a woman's wiles. Also a favorite topic of Israelite narrative art, this motif consists of: (1) a woman's feigned friendship or love; (2) a hero's submission to the woman's advances; (3) flirtatious teasing and tearful imploring; (4) a woman's victory over the hero. Elements of this powerful interplay of forces occur in the stories about Jael, Esther and Judith.

In the account of Deborah and Barak's victory over Jabin and Sisera, preserved in both a prose and a poetic version, Sisera sought refuge from Jael, the wife of Heber the Kenite. Clan loyalty weighed more heavily in her thoughts than the obligation to protect a guest in her tent. Feigning friendship, she offered him sustenance and safe lodging. Sisera submitted to her, and slept peacefully until she drove a tent peg into his skull (Judges 4—5).

One of the scenes recorded in the Book of Esther contains this motif of an endangered hero in distorted form.[35] Esther pretended to take special delight in Haman, the archenemy of the Jews, and invited him to a banquet on two successive nights. On the occasion of the second banquet the king offered her anything she wanted up to half the kingdom, as he had done the first night. Whereupon Esther identified Haman as her foe and sealed his fate.

The Book of Judith[36] also makes use of the motif of an

endangered hero in a woman's clutches. The beautiful widow abandoned her beseiged town in search of excitement, so it seemed. Her journey took her to the camp of Holofernes, the general of the Assyrian army, who fell victim to her charm. Judith offered him her "love" and Holofernes submitted to her. When the occasion arose, she cut off his head and took it with her to show her people that all danger had passed.

The fullest account of this motif occurs in the Samson saga. Besides the feigned love, the hero's submission, and the woman's victory it makes use of an element of suspense missing from the other stories. Here Samson teased Delilah, as it were, playing with fire until inevitably its flame devoured him. Such teasing does not occur in the other three accounts, unless Esther's treatment of Haman falls into this category. If so, the narrator has transformed that particular component of the motif completely, for here the woman teases the powerful hero.

The Samson narrative employs the motif twice, although this double usage required considerable alteration in the constituent parts. The description of his relationship with the beautiful Timnite varies the motif at one decisive stage—the destruction of the hero. In keeping with the narrator's fondness for suspense, the story anticipates a subsequent encounter with a dangerous woman. Hence this brief episode with the Timnite woman describes proffered love to the hero, submission to the woman, vexatious imploring on her part to discover something of value, and the loss of a great treasure, the wife.

Quest for a Deity's Name

A third motif within the Samson saga concerns the quest for a deity's name.[37] In the ancient world names reflected character.[38] Numerous biblical stories attest to the care with which Israelites chose a name for a person that accurately signified his or her real identity. The Book of Ruth richly illustrates this concern for bestowing appropriate names upon persons. The names given Naomi's two sons, Mahlon and Chilion, reflect their frailty and sickness that eventuate in early death. Similarly, Naomi's bitter experience belied the name bestowed upon her, for the loss of sons and husband was hardly "pleas-ant." Thus her request to be called *Mara* (bitter) arose from a keen sense of appropriateness in nomenclature.

Inasmuch as names reflected character, divine names sig-nified a people's experience of that deity's true nature. Knowl-edge of God's name implied a relationship of reciprocity. In time ritual use of special names for gods became a valuable means of safeguarding life. Thus the belief arose that knowl-edge of a deity's name bestowed power over that deity upon the lucky person. Accordingly, gods guarded their true identity lest their names be profaned and supplication become constant.

Several stories tell about God's appearance to someone who requests his name, only to be told that such knowledge is not forthcoming. The deity does, nevertheless, provide a clue as to his name, and the person so honored worships God according to the information divulged. In some versions of the motif a hostile God manifests himself; in others, a messenger of God evokes proper awe.

Jacob's terrifying encounter with a man bent on destroying him has a double query about the identity of assailant and victim (Genesis 32:22–32). Although the man refused to iden-tify himself in the way Jacob had readily done, he did change Jacob's name to Israel (He who strives with God, or God strives). In this new name Jacob discovered a decisive clue about the identity of his opponent, and called the place Peniel in honor of God whom he had seen face to face.

A similar desire to discover God's name fills the narrative of God's initial appearance to Moses (Exodus 3:1—4:17). Here again the deity refused to oblige the petitioner, but offered a clue that preserved his holiness and at the same time assured Moses of his constant concern. The much discussed divine re-sponse, "I AM WHO I AM," contains a word play on the special name Yahweh, which is here associated with the verb *hayah* (to be).

The angel's appearance to Manoah[39] evoked a request for his identity that would have been more appropriate to a stam-mering Moses. In any case, Manoah's syntax faltered in the presence of this wondrous visitor who had brought such joyous news.[40] "Who . . . your name?" hardly passes for correct linguistic usage. True to form, the angel refused to supply the missing data, but offered instead a clue to that valuable knowledge. Manoah seized the clue and interpreted it like a true sage, demonstrating that newfound knowledge in the act of sacrifice and in his choice of offerings. *explain*

To sum up, the motif of a quest for the divine name includes (1) a divine manifestation; (2) a human request for the God's name; (3) a divine refusal, together with a gift of a clue as to the concealed name; and (4) the successful use of that clue.

The Death Wish of a Hero

Samson's flirtation with disaster almost constitutes a death wish.[41] This motif becomes explicit in the Samson saga as a direct result of his encounter with Delilah. Finding the burden of bondage to darkness and a lifelong foe unbearable, the unfortunate Samson used the festive, sporting occasion to take his own life. But he first made supplication to God.

The Samson narrative's use of the death wish differs greatly from its other expressions in biblical literature. In these stories four elements always appear: (1) someone finds himself or herself in desperate straits; (2) she or he requests death from God; (3) the deity sustains or reasons with the person asking to die; (4) he or she chooses to continue living. In this regard, Samson's suicide breaks out of the customary form, but his departure was presaged in at least one of the death wishes we shall consider.

That narrative occurs in the Elijah cycle. The prophet's remarkable victory over Baal's prophets scarcely afforded a moment's relaxation, for Jezebel swore to kill him within twenty-four hours. The distance that he managed to put between himself and Jezebel did not suffice to overcome Elijah's desire to die. So he sat down under a tree and asked to die, since he was no better than his fathers. During the night an angel made two visits to him, bringing food and water both times, and urging him to eat lest the coming journey be too much for him. That journey behind him, Elijah confronted God in a stillness that followed earthquake, wind and fire. This God put Elijah to

work; at the same time, he instructed Elijah to anoint his
successor. In this instance, a short delay occurred in the fulfillment of the prophet's death wish (1 Kings 19:1–18).

Divine compassion for a great city of repentant foreigners
prompted Jonah's death wish. His own reputation for accuracy
of prediction shattered by God's repentance of an earlier decision to destroy Nineveh, Jonah reasoned with God in such a
way as to demonstrate the selfishness of his actions. Since he
knew that God was "a gracious God and merciful, slow to anger,
and abounding in steadfast love, and repentest of evil," knowledge gained from familiarity with the story of God's appearance to Moses (Exodus 34:1–9), Jonah had earlier fled from God.
Unable to tolerate such a God, Jonah begged him to take his
life, "for it is better for me to die than to live." Whereupon God
reasoned with Jonah, and furnished an object lesson that was
construed to teach the sulking prophet the error of his ways.
Jonah persisted in his anger, which he thought justified the
death wish, and God explained the meaning of the object lesson
that had not been transparent to Jonah. Though the text leaves
Jonah chafing from God's rebuke, one can suppose that the
prophet abandoned his death wish. On the other hand, nothing
demands such a favorable interpretation of Jonah's fate.[42]

The Book of Tobit juxtaposes two death wishes, Tobit's and
Sarah's. The devout Tobit performed an act of charity but suffered blindness as an indirect result of his deed. Physicians
could not relieve the malady, and Anna, Tobit's wife, went to
work to provide life's necessities. Tobit's sickness even affected
his judgment, and he accused his devoted wife of theft.[43] Although she returned the object in question, Anna showed herself capable of an astute assessment of her husband's character:
"Where are your charities and your righteous deeds? You seem
to know everything!" (Tobit 2:14, RSV) Her words burned into
his conscience, and Tobit prayed in great distress that God
command that Tobit's spirit be taken up and that he "depart
and become dust." Tobit, too, claimed that death was preferable
to a life characterized by reproach and sorrow. Repeating his
urgent request, Tobit prayed:

Command that I now be released from my distress to go to the
eternal abode; do not turn thy face away from me (3:6,RSV).

That very day Tobit's future daughter-in-law, Sarah, suffered reproach from her handmaids who accused Sarah of
strangling seven of her husbands on their wedding nights.
Overcome by these accusations and curses, she contemplated
suicide but dismissed it lest she bring dishonor to her father.
Turning to God in prayer, Sarah described her plight and requested release from the earth and its reproach. But she kept
alive a faint hope. In case God did not wish to take her life, she
urged him to command that respect be shown her and that
reproach be removed. God heard both prayers, and sent Ra-
phael to restore Tobit's sight, to give Sarah in marriage to
Tobias, Tobit's son, and to bind Asmodeus, the demon responsible for her trouble.

Samson's death wish coincides with only two of the main
components of these accounts: He finds himself in desperate
circumstances, and he requests death. If his final words express
defiant resignation rather than continuing his prayer, only one
of the four elements applies. Missing are God's reasoning with
the tired hero and an inference of renewed will to live.

Loss of Charisma

A fifth motif within the Samson saga, the loss of charisma,
will occupy our attention in another chapter. For the moment
we shall merely delineate its characteristics. Four things dominate the motif: (1) a hero betrays his vocation; (2) God with-
draws the blessing that accompanied his special calling; (3)
adversity stalks the bygone hero; (4) death occurs at the hands
of enemies.

Outside the Samson narrative, this motif, the loss of charisma, dominates the account of Saul's last days. As penalty for
failing to obey Samuel's instructions, and also for assuming
priestly functions, Saul betrays his calling to rule over Israel
and loses divine favor. Thereafter David's star begins to rise,
and Saul suffers in mind and body. In the end madness prevails,
and Saul seeks help from a medium. In vain, however, he turns
from the true God. Accepting his fate like a courageous soldier,

Saul goes to his death in battle against the Philistines (1 Samuel 15—31).

Terror over Theophany

The final motif that we shall consider concerns terror over a theophany.[44] In it God manifests himself, dread overwhelms the human witness to divine presence, God tempers the fear, and the recipient of God's coming becomes a changed person. In connection with our discussion of the quest for the divine name, we touched upon two stories in which the motif of terror over theophany played a decisive role. Jacob's response to the nocturnal visitor bent on conquering him at wrestling reveals the terror implicit in theophany. Upon discovering the identity of his attacker, Jacob expressed astonishment that he had seen God face to face and lived to tell about it. Concealed within this reaction lies a belief that theophany spells danger. In the other narrative, Moses received ample warning to take off his shoes in God's presence.

The parade example of the motif under discussion occurs in the account of Isaiah's call to prophesy (Isaiah 6). Here the divine appearance evoked *mysterium tremendum et fascinans,* to use Rudolf Otto's apt language.[45] Overcome by the Holy One, Isaiah cried out that his life was in jeopardy, for he had seen the King, the Lord of Hosts. An expression of divine forgiveness followed, a cleansing of Isaiah's unclean lips. Then Isaiah heard the heavenly dialogue, entered into it, and volunteered to become God's spokesman.

The story of Manoah's sacrifice to the God who performs marvelous things reflects the concerns characteristic of the motif under consideration. The angel of God appeared and manifested his awesome character by ascending to heaven in the flame from the altar. Dread overwhelmed Manoah as he gazed at the wondrous sight, and he feared death. In this instance his wife allayed Manoah's fear, assuring him that God did not intend to slay them since he had made known his will for their lives. This story remains silent about a subsequent change in Manoah's character, unless such transformation can be gleaned from his conduct in regard to Samson's desire to marry a lovely Timnite.

Stylistic Features

Thus far we have examined the traditions incorporated into the Samson saga and have looked at various motifs embodied within the story. We have said little about the literary characteristics of the narrative itself. Our present task is to describe the syntactic features of the saga, its semantic field, and its rhetorical devices.

Syntax

The Samson narrative is a good example of biblical prose, with rare poetic exceptions. Its sentence order seldom varies from the customary, and those instances function to emphasize the direct object (e.g. "For *God* we have seen"; *"her* get for me, for she pleases me"). Replete with imperfects, especially with the *waw* consecutive, the saga underscores the flow of events and thus supports the theory that one wrong begets another, which in turn gives birth to still another offense. Indicators for the direct object occur sparsely, often with pronominal objects. Few adverbs, interjections or particles appear, except in certain contexts that absolutely demand their presence. While infinitives and participles occur quite freely, imperatives seldom do. Occasionally, improper syntax crops up, but it functions ideologically. For example, Manoah's stammering question, "Who . . . your name?" gives voice to his growing awareness that the messenger who had brought such good tidings was none other than God's emissary.[46]

Semantic Field

The semantic field covers a wide range of topics. Language of love and family characterizes the first chapter; indeed, eros punctuates the total narrative. Affective terms abound, both positive and negative. Cultic language occupies an exalted position in the first episode, and crops up now and again elsewhere. And, of course, terms of conflict dominate the account of Samson's encounter with the Philistines. Animals function in a supportive role only, either to pose a test of strength, or to inflict further damage upon the uncircumcised, or even to pacify an angry bride. Clan terms appear, but play a minor role in the story. Kinship ties, on the other hand, exercise a powerful restraining force upon the story's plot. The heavens barely receive a passing nod; sun, moon, and stars determine nobody's fate in the Samson saga. That destiny rests in Samson's capable hands alone, and in the power granted him by Israel's God. Time makes its oppressive presence felt again and again; temporal references occur frequently at crucial stages of the plot. Numbers, particularly exaggerated ones, occur with regularity. Symbols hardly occur, and folk sayings find an echo in only one comment, Samson's retort to the Philistines who discovered the meaning of his clever riddle. Astonishingly, we do not encounter a curse in the entire saga. On the other hand, the Lord's blessing rested upon the lad Samson.

Rhetoric

The Samson narrative makes use of a rich fund of rhetoric,[47] which suggests that an author or authors consciously endeavored to demonstrate mastery of the art of suasion. Each stylistic feature was chosen because of its remarkable power to move hearers to admiration and action. Whether the device looked forward to coming attractions or glanced backward at what had already been spoken; whether it slowed down the pace of the story or heightened suspense; whether it seized the moment to invoke laughter, or carried the argument to the ludicrous; whether it painted contrasting pictures, or burst with powerful dialogue and its correlate, monologue—the stylistic feature enhanced the artistry of the saga. We turn now to examine this exquisite art.

Anticipation

The Samson saga is rich in anticipation. The author provides a preview of coming attractions, alerting the audience or reader to future occurrence of the idea and assuring unity of plot. The opening verse speaks about *the hand of the Philistines* as divine punishment. The heavenly messenger picks up this idea in his prediction that Samson would begin to deliver Israel from the hand of the Philistines, and a thirsty warrior grasps those words again to describe the threat to his survival. Once Samson actually falls into the power of his enemy, the narrator dispenses with the phrase in favor of description itself.

Similarly, the identity of Yahweh's angel is anticipated by Manoah's wife, as it were, intuitively; her description of the messenger's awesome appearance like that of the angel of God points forward to Manoah's shocking discovery of this reality. Whereas she did not presume to ask him his name, Manoah does precisely that. Her remark to Manoah, "I did not ask him where he came from, and he did not tell me *his name,*" lights a small flame that eventuates in the altar fire and its accompanying query, "Who . . . your name?"

Samson's dangerous teasing of Delilah alludes to the departure of his strength if Delilah does a prescribed thing. Once she carried out the instructions, the Lord departed from Samson. As a consequence of Delilah's oppressive words, Samson became *impatient to die.* Later, when lust for revenge consumed him, Samson *desired to die* with the Philistines. The thirty guests at Samson's wedding threatened to *burn the Timnite and her father's house* if she failed to obtain vital information for them. In retaliation for Samson's mischief with the foxes, the Philistines *burned her and her father.* The Philistines stood Samson between the *columns;* Samson later put his strategic location to effective use.

One can even speak of anticipation when the actual word or phrase occurs only once. For instance, the allusion to Samson's beginning to deliver Israel looks forward to his wondrous exploits, and beyond them, to subsequent warriors who will bring the battle to its final stages. Likewise the reference to renewed growth of Samson's hair presages ill for those who precipitated Samson's breach of the Nazirite vow.

Repetition

In a sense, anticipation and repetition belong together, for a word or phrase occurs early in an account and then appears at a later time. Repetition differs, however, in its function. Whereas anticipation hastens the narrative to its denouement, repetition slows down the narrative and heightens suspense. Still, many cases of repetition resemble those already discussed under anticipation, for reiteration functions in ways other than to retard the movement of a story. The lovely Timnite was *right in Samson's eyes*, so much so that the fact receives double mention. On the other hand, the two scandalous stories that follow the Samson narrative contain a framing motto that emphasizes every person's acting according to what was right in his or her eyes.[48] Thus repetition within a narrative functions as anticipation when viewed from the broader perspective.

Repetition fills the Samson saga from beginning to end. The angel's greeting to Manoah's wife, "Behold, you are barren and have no child," and his instructions to her, "Do not let him drink wine or fermented drink, nor eat anything unclean" are repeated, the former for her sake and the latter for Manoah's. The messenger's characterization of the lad as a Nazirite of God from the womb becomes in the woman's mouth, "For the lad will be a Nazirite of God from the womb *until the day of his death.*"[49] Here anticipation and repetition meet once again.

Sometimes the repetition constitutes a formula or refrain. For example, the same formula tells of Samson's discovery of the lovely Timnite and the harlot at Gaza. It reads: "And Samson went down to Timnah/Gaza and saw a woman in Timnah/there." Differences occur within the formula, however. The first reference identifies the woman as one of the Philistine daughters; the second qualifies the woman by the term, harlot. Furthermore, Samson went down *(yarad)* to Timnah, and went *(halak)* to Gaza.

The Delilah episode makes copious use of refrains: "wherein his strength is great and in what way he can be bound so that one can afflict him"; "I shall become weak and be like every man"; "the Philistines were waiting in the inner room"; "the Philistines are upon you, Samson"; "and his strength was not known"; "he told her all his mind." So, too, the final drama repeats the reference to the columns upon which the building rested; the droning of this expansive vocabulary approaches a refrain leading to the final collapse of those columns.

Repetition spans the entire saga, overlapping the several episodes. The Philistine imperative to the Timnite, "Entice your husband," does double duty, for the lords of the Philistines instruct Delilah to "entice him." In both instances the enticement *vexed* Samson, whether by tears or pleas. Similarly, Samson found himself in the same predicament that his father had encountered—both lacked crucial data. "Now Manoah did not know that he was the angel of the Lord" corresponds to "For he (Samson) did not know that the Lord had departed from him."[50] The former narrative hastens to add, "Then Manoah knew that he was the angel of the Lord," but Samson's knowledge assumes a much more gruesome form and must be inferred. His loss of sight and freedom implied divine abandonment, necessitating a prayer for remembrance.

Retardation and Restraint

The observation that Manoah did not know that his visitor was the Lord's angel functions to retard the movement of the story and to relieve tension by reminding hearers or readers of the gap between then and now. The author or editor has scattered several such comments here and there in the saga. Thus we read: "Now his father and mother did not know that it was from the Lord, for he wished to seek (an affront) from the Philistines. At that time Philistines were ruling over Israel." Or again we hear, "for so the young men used to do" and "therefore he called its name *En Haqqore'* which is in *Lehi* until this day."

The account of the disappearance of the angel while *Manoah and his wife looked on* (repeated twice to emphasize the awefulness of the occasion) and the narrative of Samson's dallying with Delilah function to retard the progress of the story. Restraint occurs, appropriately exercized by Manoah's wife, who refuses to pry when glad tidings have put an end to her reproach.

Assonance

The saga uses assonance sparingly, in accord with its prose form. Brief poetic formulations within the narrative do utilize puns and, surprisingly, rhyme. Samson's victory chant plays on

—we hesitate to call it assonance—the word for ass, chiefly by a fourfold usage. The Philistines' victory song makes extraordinary use of rhyme, the eightfold occurrence of the first person plural pronominal ending. The report that Samson gave a feast at Timnah constitutes a "clever play on the sibilants" *(wayyá ʿas sham shimshón mishtéh),*[51] and the first two riddles abound in initial "m" sounds (nine in twelve words, if we disregard the conjunction). We have already pointed out the pun on "thirst" and "find" in connection with the aetiology of the Partridge Spring. We note further that the place name Ramath-lehi is echoed in the immediate sequel, which reports that Samson came alive *(wayyechi).*

Contrast

Contrast contributes richly to the delineation of character within the story. Love and hate, friend and foe, strength and weakness, knowledge and ignorance, joy and sorrow punctuate the narrative. This contrast stands out most effectively in the choice of verbs that describe Samson's journeys from one place to another. Use of *yarad* (to go down) and *ʿalah* (to go up) in crucial scenes suggests conscious structuring, and perhaps even a symbolic sense for both. *Yarad* refers to: Samson's trip to Timnah (four times); his journey to Askelon; his flight to the crag at Etam; the visit by three thousand Philistines (twice); the return trip to Gaza; and the last journey by Samson's brothers and kinsmen in search of his corpse for proper burial. *ʿalah* plays an even greater role in the story. It occurs in reference to: a razor coming upon Samson's head (twice); the angel's departure in a flame; Samson's return to his parents (twice); the Philistines' hasty trip to burn the Timnite family; the Philistine invasion of Judah (three times); the men of Judah's purpose in coming to Samson in hiding; Samson's jaunt with Gaza's gate and posts on his shoulders; the Philistine lords' visit of Delilah (five times); and the quest for Samson's body.

In light of this total contrast of verbs we may ascribe greater significance to direct expressions of opposites. For example, in the first situation below, the flame joins two opposites, heaven and earth. In any event, mediation of opposites or at least of contrasting concepts takes place. Within chapter thirteen alone the following occur:

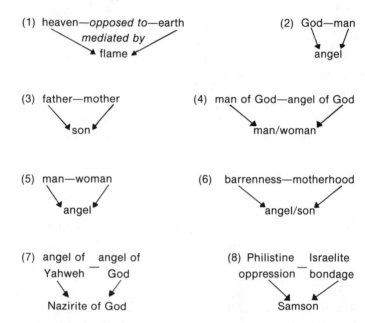

(1) heaven—*opposed to*—earth
       mediated by
       ▲ flame ◄

(2) God—man
     angel

(3) father—mother
   son

(4) man of God—angel of God
    man/woman

(5) man—woman
   angel

(6) barrenness—motherhood
    angel/son

(7) angel of angel of
   Yahweh ‾ God
   Nazirite of God

(8) Philistine Israelite
   oppression ‾ bondage
    Samson

"Pregnant" Terms

Certain expressions within the Samson narrative are brimming with implication; hence we call these "pregnant" terms. For instance, the angel's prediction that Samson would *begin* to deliver Israel from the hand of the Philistines employs the word *yachel*. This verb occurs four times in the saga, each time in crucial settings and with different infinitival objects. The other three uses refer to the initial stirring of the lad ("The spirit of the Lord began to stir him at Mahaneh-dan"), Delilah's first afflicting of Samson after she had shaven his head, and the renewal of his hair's growth. The four uses of *yachel* form an inclusio of sorts. The first and last abort in the story; only the second and third accomplish their desired goals.

Other expressions belong to the same category and justify the description, "pregnant" terms. We shall discuss the full weight of these in later chapters where the relevant texts are examined. For the present it suffices to mention them. They include: Samson's mother's addition to the angel's message ("until the day of his death"); the Judahites' question addressed to Samson ("Do you not know that the Philistines rule over us?"); the identification of Samson's loss of strength with the Lord's departure; Samson's resolve to get revenge once and to stop afterwards; the allusion to making sport; the angel's clever use of a play on words for "entreat" earlier addressed to the Lord (*'atsar*-tread/*'atar*-entreat).

Humor

Lacking the benefit of intonation and accompanying gestures, the identification of humor[52] in ancient texts is notoriously difficult. What strikes modern readers as outrageously funny may not have elicited the faintest smile from ancient audiences, and something wholly ludicrous to them may appear entirely appropriate to us. Still we hazard the claim that certain elements in the Samson saga are inherently funny. Into this category falls Samson's method of setting fire to enemy grain fields; the possibility that an ancient ritual for preventing mildew stands behind the story hardly negates its humorous quality. Likewise Samson's postcoital activity must have brought hearty laughter to ancient listeners and readers. The visual image of one who has spent half the night with a harlot emerging from that encounter with strength sufficient to carry heavy posts and a gate for over forty miles surely evoked snickers if not boisterous response.[53] Perhaps Samson's side trip to take a look at a dead carcass while on his way to marry the beautiful Timnite who had so captivated him also belongs to the category of the humorous.[54]

Hyperbole

An essential characteristic of legend, hyperbole, occurs often in the Samson narrative. Exaggeration of numbers, distances, and deeds takes place, for anything can happen in legends. Accordingly, Samson slays a thousand people with the jawbone of an ass, or catches three hundred foxes, or withstands three thousand Judahites, or kills three thousand Philistines in one building.[55] In short, hyperbole has penetrated the saga from its inception. It suffuses the accounts of the Timnite's beauty, Samson's victory over a lion, the amount of silver paid to Delilah, and every experience the hero undergoes, whether positive or negative.

Dialogue and Monologue

Lively dialogue enriches the Samson narrative, providing a good balance to the violent activity recounted. In every case the dialogue is brief and to the point, thereby offering characterization without impeding the progress of the story. By means of such dialogue the author has brought his readers into the action of the story, whether the conversation be between a woman and an angel, a man and his wife, parents and their son, two lovers, inveterate foes, clansmen, a hero and his God, or a prisoner and his youthful guide.

Monologue takes place in the story as well. Curiously, it always aborts. Monologue occurs only in those places where someone expresses an intention that is later frustrated. On three different occasions Samson uttered a monologue of this kind. He expressed his intention of going in to his wife, only to have his father-in-law prevent such action. Samson promised himself that he would take revenge this once, and afterwards would quit; but the Philistines refused to rest until they had obtained redress for wrongs committed against them. After Samson lost his precious locks of hair, he awoke with confidence and muttered to himself that he would shake himself free and go out as usual. This time he could not throw off the bonds. Samson's were not the only monologues that aborted. The Gazites who lay in wait for Samson gave voice to a "collective" monologue: "At the crack of dawn we will kill him." By that hour of the day Samson was far away with his unusual burden, and the Gazites perceived the folly of their plan.

Suspense

When the audience knows the plot, a storyteller must strive mightily to sustain suspense. The Samson saga achieves a high degree of suspense in the Delilah episode, largely through the use of refrains (cf. especially "The Philistines are upon you,

Samson"). One can even explain the reference to the regrowth of Samson's hair as a suspense-creator; thus the failure of the story to make use of the idea later becomes understandable. The allusion to Samson's hair beginning to grow functioned solely to create suspense. Perhaps, too, the reference to Gazites lying in wait while Samson, wholly unaware of their presence, cavorted with a harlot evoked suspense. But one did not have to wait long to find out Samson's fate.

So far we have examined the traditions incorporated into the Samson saga, the motifs employed, the heroic exploits celebrated, and have analyzed the syntactic, semantic, and rhetorical features of the narrative. We turn now to take a look at the larger setting within which the Samson stories have been placed.

The Larger Context

The Samson narrative appears within the Book of Judges. The latter consists of a series of stories describing major and minor judges who functioned during the period beginning with Israel's entry into Canaan and ending with the anointing of Saul as king in Israel. In those days when there was no king in Israel and every man did what was right in his own eyes, life was perilous indeed. Deliverers rose up to defend various clans from their oppressors. To these valiant soldiers the title *shophet* was given.[56] Basically, two kinds of judges functioned in behalf of the Israelites.[57] The "minor" judges proclaimed divine law and sought to implement its stipulations among the people. Major judges, on the other hand, fought in behalf of a beleaguered tribe to throw off the yoke of foreign oppression.

Samson belongs to the latter type of judge. But his actions differ radically from those of his fellow judges in one significant respect. Whereas they fought for the wellbeing of clans, Samson's exploits constitute a personal vendetta against the Philistines. The major judges' military forays undertake to rescue a people and to restore their dignity; Samson fights to extricate himself from a trap he inadvertently laid, or to avenge wrongs brought on by his own folly.

Each major judge arose in response to external oppression.

Othniel defeated Cushan-risathaim, king of Mesopotamia, whom the Israelites had served for eight years. The Moabites suppressed Israel for eighteen years, until Ehud came to her rescue. Shamgar slew six hundred Philistines with an oxgoad, thereby delivering Israel for a season. Canaanite oppression called forth a joint effort by Deborah and Barak, whose coalition of volunteers routed the army of Jabin and Sisera. Gideon's select few put to flight the entire Midianite force, and thus rid the land of marauders bent on harvesting Israelite crops. Jephthah delivered Israel from the threat of Ammonite rule; in return he became sole ruler in Gilead.

These stories reflect a particular view of history. The nation that forgets God suffers duress from foreign powers. A repentant people receives divine deliverance. This interpretation of human events characterizes the Book of Deuteronomy, as well as Joshua, Judges, Samuel, and Kings. According to the spirit that pervades these writings, history teaches a moral lesson. Presumably, this view controls the selection of episodes that make up the Book of Judges, and determines the features to be stressed. Everything that failed to fit the pattern was discarded.

Given the emphasis placed on the gift of the land in other Israelite traditions, the author faced two puzzling facts. In reality the conquest of Palestine took decades, and was the result of gradual intermingling with the indigenous population. Moreover, the people of God suffered at the hands of various powers for over two centuries. How could these things be if the exodus from Egypt were really what tradition proclaimed? As supplied by the author of Judges, the answer to the dilemma posed by stark reality appears in 2:6—3:6. A new generation arose who did not know the marvelous work of the Lord, and who gave their allegiance to alien gods. In anger Yahweh gave them into the hand of plunderers, but heeding their cry he raised up judges to deliver them. Inconstant, the people turned to other gods after each judge's death. God determined to test his people by means of foreign powers. Certain nations were thus allowed to remain in Palestine. So Joshua did not conquer the Philistines, Canaanites, Sidonians, and the Hivites. Israel failed the test, particularly in the area of intermarriage. One outcome of such unions was the adoption of religious allegiance. The sons and daughters who married the Canaanites, Hittites, Amorites, Perizzites, Hivites and Jebusites served their gods.

As a consequence of this response to the delay in possessing the land and the long struggle against oppressors, local heroes are transformed into deliverers of all Israel, and the impression is given that judges arose in succession. Those who actually functioned during the same general period but in localized clans have been placed within an artificial setting, and their exploits have been stretched to embrace all Israel. As a result, we can no longer determine the exact chronology of the incidents preserved.

The author's realization of the disparity between hallowed tradition and reality surfaces again in the story of Yahweh's angel's appearance to Gideon. Hardly impressed by the angel's greeting that the Lord is with him, a sceptical Gideon responded: "Pray, sir, if the Lord is with us, why then has all this befallen us? And where are all his wonderful deeds which our fathers recounted to us, saying, 'Did not the Lord bring us up from Egypt?' But now the Lord has cast us off, and given us into the hand of Midian" (6:13, RSV).

In one other significant area of Israel's life anticipation often exceeded actual reality. The author incorporates two stories that defend the institution of kingship, albeit indirectly. He surrounds each with a summary judgment: "In those days there was no king in Israel; every man did what was right in his own eyes" (17:6; 21:25; cf. 18:1; 19:1). The first story concerns an untrustworthy Levite, the second a Levite's concubine.

In the hill country of Ephraim a man named Micah stole eleven hundred pieces of silver from his mother, but returned it after she pronounced a curse upon the thief. The mother dedicated the money to the Lord; from it Micah constructed a graven image, a molten image, an ephod and teraphim. At first he installed one of his sons as priest, but subsequently em-

ployed a Levite who had journeyed from Bethlehem to
Ephraim. While searching for a land in which to settle their
clan, five Danites enlisted an oracle from the Levite. Since the
word was favorable, they journeyed to Laish and discovered
there a people who dwelt to themselves. Some time later six
hundred soldiers from the tribe of Dan came back to Micah's
house, stole his image and persuaded the Levite to accompany
them. Having burned the city of Laish, the Danites rebuilt it,
named it Dan, and set up the graven image they had stolen.

Another Levite sojourned in the hill country of Ephraim
and took a concubine from Bethlehem. In anger she ran away
to her home in Bethlehem. Four months later her husband
went for her, and drank heartily for days with the father-in-
law. On the fifth day he and his concubine departed late in the
afternoon and arrived opposite Jebus, that is, Jerusalem, at
nightfall. Rejecting his servant's advice to spend the night at
Jebus, a city occupied by foreigners, the Levite journeyed to
Gibeah and turned aside there among the Benjaminites. The
people of Gibeah ignored the Levite, until finally an old man
from the hill country of Ephraim who was sojourning at Gibeah
took him in for the night. Later that evening base men came
to obtain the Levite for homosexual purposes. The old man
offered them his virgin daughter and the concubine, but urged
them not to abuse the Levite. So the man seized his concubine
and put her out to them. Weakened from a full night's abuse,
she came at dawn and fell down at the door of the house in
which her master slept peacefully. In preparing to depart, he
discovered his concubine's body at the door and ordered her to
get up. When she did not answer, he put her on his ass and
returned home. Whereupon he divided her into twelve pieces
and sent them throughout the territory of Israel. The representatives of the people assembled and decided to punish Gibeah for this heinous crime. Fierce fighting ensued, and the
tribe of Benjamin was nearly exterminated. Reason prevailed,
and special means were devised to secure wives for the few
surviving Benjaminites lest the tribe vanish. It was determined
that the inhabitants of Jabesh-gilead failed to attend the assembly at Mizpah in response to the Levite's bloody message.

As punishment, the city was razed. Only four hundred young virgins were spared. These were given to the survivors of Benjamin, but did not suffice. Since the Israelites had pronounced a curse upon anyone who gives his daughter to a Benjaminite, they decided to permit Benjaminites to attend the annual festival at Shiloh and to seize any daughter of Shiloh who came out to dance. In this way the tribe of Benjamin replenished itself.

We noted earlier that the Samson saga and the Samuel narrative once formed a larger account in which each hero judged Israel twenty years for a total of forty years during Philistine rule. How can we explain the obvious intrusion of these scandalous stories into the Book of Judges?

At least three observations seem appropriate. First, Micah belonged to the tribe of Dan, whose most celebrated member was Samson. Now Samson's activity appears to have taken place after the Danite migration to northern Palestine, certain members of the clan having remained at the site of the original settlement of the group.[58] If so, the story about Micah and the Levite should precede the Samson narrative chronologically. Second, the exorbitant bribe offered and delivered by each Philistine lord to Delilah corresponds to the amount of silver that Micah stole from his mother. Perhaps this fact also brought the two stories together. Third, the scandalous stories belong to the period of the judges. Accordingly, someone appended them to the account of the last great judge after Samuel came to be viewed as more than a judge.

The Book of Judges belongs to a larger literary context, identified above as entities controlled by a special view of history. These four books, Joshua through Kings in the Hebrew canon, make up the Former Prophets. Together with Isaiah, Jeremiah, Ezekiel and the Twelve they compose the second division of the canon, the $n^e bi'im$. The Samson narrative fits rather badly in a canonical context, causing considerable embarrassment for some commentators.[59] However offensive to later sensibilities, these stories arose in a society that appreciated them for their narrative power. The saga gave voice to aspirations of better things at a time when Israel had little else to boast about.

So far we have carefully avoided the matter of date. When did the saga come into existence? If one could assume that the core of the narrative has historicity, it would be natural to date the original traditions during the period of Philistine hegemony over Israel, and to view them as spontaneous creations by a people who acknowledged Samson as judge. One could then argue that subsequent editors have touched up the stories and given them a distinctive point of view.

On the other hand, the Samson narrative contains little that can definitely be called historical. Nothing requires a date during the pre-monarchical period; indeed, certain comments demand a considerably later date for the story *in its present form*. In all probability the stories antedate the Deuteronomistic history, of which they form a part. Further precision in dating them can scarcely be offered.

If the claim that the Samson narrative contains evidence of the Yahwistic and Elohistic strands of the Pentateuch were correct,[60] it would probably necessitate a considerably earlier date for the saga. Unfortunately, stylistic affinities with these two streams of tradition hardly imply the separate existence of two Samson stories. Nor does the presence of two summary statements point to dual sources, since one summary may have accompanied an aetiology that had been joined to the Samson saga by that means. Rejection of spiritual passages in the saga as secondary lacks cogency, resting as it does upon a prior understanding of the development of Israel's literature and religion.[61] Even the birth story cannot be excluded from the original saga without doing injustice to numerous indications of unity, particularly in substance.

In short, I view the saga as legendary and of uncertain date. In my view, its purpose is two-fold: to provide entertainment and to offer negative example. The story entertains and teaches. Where it contains history, that element is incidental to the story's purpose. I shall attempt to elucidate that purpose in the following chapter.

Chapter Two
Passion or Charisma?

Unifying Themes

The Samson saga entertains and teaches. But what message does it communicate? Perhaps we should recognize more than one aim in a story as complex as this one. I believe the primary purpose of the saga was to examine competing loyalties.[1] On one level, it addresses the tension between filial devotion and erotic attachment, thus providing a sort of midrash on the astute observation in Genesis 2:24 ("Therefore a man leaves his father and his mother and cleaves to his wife, and they become one flesh."—RSV). On another level, the saga offers a negative example that calls attention to a broken vow and its consequences.[2] In this chapter we shall consider the first purpose. Chapter four will take up the matter of a broken vow.

We take our clue to the principal purpose of the narrative from Samson's reply to the Timnite woman who accused him of deficiency in love. Juxtaposing a positive and a negative for emphasis, she makes her point most tellingly: "You only hate me. You don't love me. You have told a riddle to my countrymen, but you have not told it to me." Samson's reply brings into sharp focus competing allegiances:

> Lo, my father and my mother I have not told (it), and I shall tell *you?* (14:16b)

We could even translate Samson's response as an expression of determination: "Behold, I haven't told my father or mother, and I won't tell you." Either translation correctly renders the Hebrew. The former assumes rising inflection in Samson's

voice, and turns the final two words into a question even without the customary sign of an interrogative. The alternative
rendering assumes that the negative in the first clause does
double duty. Regardless of the translation, the contest between
parents and bride could hardly be made more effectively.

How should we interpret her accusation? On the face of it,
she seems to say that she has not even heard the riddle, much
less its interpretation. What had Samson kept from his parents? According to 14:6b, he did not tell his parents about
killing a lion on the way to Timnah, and 14:9 reports that he
didn't tell them that the honey he gave them came from the
carcass of that lion. In short, Samson withheld from his parents
crucial data that would enable them to interpret his riddle.
Perhaps one should assume that such action on his part arose
from a desire to protect them from Philistines seeking to un-
ravel his riddle. In any case, Samson had kept his secret from
his parents, and the lovely Timnite inquired about the riddle
and its meaning. Since she was able to tell the Philistines the
interpretation of Samson's riddle, she sought and obtained
more than the actual riddle.

Samson's question addressed to a pouting bride articulates
the leitmotif of the saga. To whom does one owe primary allegiance—parents, or lover? Affection for parents suddenly faces
rival attraction, evoking rash conduct and stern language to an
aging father. Caught up in the surge of erotic desire, Samson
asserts his rights and determines to have his way. Now he
questions his rashness, and defends himself by appealing to a
reality that he had put in jeopardy—a close bond with his
parents. Samson's reply to his bride poses the issue in its stark-
est form. If I have not told my riddle to my father and mother,
do you actually think I will tell it to you? Do you believe a few
days in your arms have given you a status in my life that
exceeds that of my parents? Under a barrage of tears, Samson's
resolve fails, and he experiences love's power and cruelty.

The thesis that Samson's reply to his bride constitutes the
theme of the saga receives support from the use of the verb tell
(ngd) throughout the narrative. Ordinary vocabulary functions

in an extraordinary fashion, providing structural unity to the entire saga.

In the first episode, the birth announcement and accompanying recognition scene, the root *ngd,* occurs in a crucial context that unites the two scenes. The barren wife of Manoah reports her reticence about asking the bearer of good tidings too many questions.

> A man of God came to me, and his countenance was like the appearance of God's angel, exceedingly awesome. I did not ask him where he came from, and he did not *tell* me his name *(lo' higgid li)* (13:6).

Manoah did not share his wife's caution, but boldly put the question of his name to the messenger, who offered a hint that would answer both questions. In contrast to the angel's reticence about his origin, Manoah's wife proclaimed everything to her husband *(wattagged).*

The second episode makes rich use of the root *ngd.* Samson informed *(wayyagged,* with numerous manuscripts) his parents of his intention to marry the Timnite, thus paving the way for a concatenation of uses in the account of that wedding. Twice the refrain occurs: "But he didn't *tell* his father or his mother" what he had done (14:6), that he had taken the honey from the lion's carcass (14:9). Rather than seeing these verses as clumsy glosses, we should recognize their function in the plot. In short, they make the point that Samson alone holds the key that unlocks the door to his riddle. Therefore Samson's request that the thirty Philistines tell him the answer to the riddle (14: 12–14) is entirely appropriate. Perhaps Samson's double use of the root *ngd* in 14:12 approaches mockery: "If you can *actually tell* it to me during the seven days of the feast and find it out . . . ." The thirty Philistines borrow Samson's language and try it on his bride: "Entice your husband and *tell* us the riddle, lest we burn you and your father's house with fire" (14:15). The pathos of the bride fills her desperate accusation:

> You only hate me, you do not love me; you have put a riddle to my countrymen, and you have not *told* it to me (14:16).

Samson's reply that he had not told it to his parents and would not tell her hardly suffices. With masterful understatement the narrative continues:

> Now she wept before him the seven[3] days of the feast, and on the seventh day he *told* her because she wearied him. Then she *told* the riddle to her countrymen (14:17).

The final use of *ngd* in this episode shifts to the thirty Philistines who *told* the riddle, thus subtly proclaiming their victory over Samson. We note a remarkable silence about this word in the Philistines' jubilant announcement of their discovery (14:18) and in Samson's bawdy reply, which returns to his original amplification of *ngd*.

> Had you not plowed with my heifer, you would not have *found out (lo' m^{e}tsa' tem)* my riddle (14:18).

The episode of the Gazite harlot continues this silence, with a single exception. This time the subject is impersonal. Someone, it matters not who, told the Gazites that Samson had come into their midst (16:2, with the Septuagint). Such careful avoidance of the root *ngd* in the story describing the ramifications of Samson's riddle contest, even in a context where one would expect it to occur (15:6), and the substitution of dialogue, suggest that we should expect lively discourse in the next use of the word.

In the fourth episode Delilah wasted no time getting around to the term *ngd*.

> Please *tell* me wherein your strength is great, and how you may be bound so as to afflict you (16:6).

On four different occasions she pleaded with her captive lover to tell her the secret of his strength, and chided him three times for *speaking (watt^{e}dabber)* lies and mocking her (16:6, 10, 13, 15). Unable to withstand her counter-speech, Samson unlocked the door to his mystery and told her all his heart (16:17), because she vexed him relentlessly with her words until he was loath to live.

The twofold use of this word *ngd* in Delilah's final appearance in the story underscores its prominence.

> When Delilah saw that he had *told* her all his heart,[4] she sent
> and summoned the Philistine lords, saying "Come up at once,
> for he has *told* me all his heart." (16:18)

Significantly, Samson fared no better under a barrage of words
than he did when flooded with tears. Both weapons wielded by
desirable women found their mark; both resulted in a twofold
telling. One, Samson's, was spoken in full trust; the other constituted outright betrayal.

The underside of this important word requires brief elucida-
tion. The urgent request that Samson *tell* his secret assumes
ignorance on the part of the petitioner. Accordingly, a refrain
functions to emphasize such absence of vital information (*lo'
yada'* and its variants). In 13:16 Manoah's boldness in questioning the angel of God evokes an explanation that Manoah did
not know that he was an angel of the Lord. Similarly, 14:4
speaks of the old man's ignorance about the real motivation for
Samson's attraction to a Timnite beauty. The infatuation came
from the Lord, who was eager to do battle with the Philistines.
Both references to Manoah's inadequate knowledge accentuate
the theological dimension of the saga, but do not for that reason
demand a theory of redaction.

In 15:11 the Judahites ask Samson whether he knows the
facts of life or not:

Do you not know that Philistines rule over us?

Whereas Manoah's ignorance concerned religious factors, Samson's touched upon political reality. Delilah, too, had deficient
knowledge in one decisive matter. Thus the story describes the
effect of her first failure to discover that datum as follows:

So (the secret of) his strength was not known (*lo' noda'*,
16:9).

Her fourth attempt succeeded, and the narrator affords us fleeting entry into Samson's inmost thoughts:

> "I shall go forth this time as before, and shake myself free
> (16:20).

Over against this audacious, ill-informed boast stands the narrator's report that "he did not know that the Lord had departed
from him" (16:20).

Women in the Samson Saga

If we are correct in viewing competing loyalties as the saga's essential theme, a thesis that seems to be confirmed by structural unity, we should be able to discern various types of relationships within the several episodes of the story. Our search for such paradigms comes off successfully, for the saga treats a different type of relationship in each of the four episodes.

The first unit (13:1–25) depicts an ideal Israelite woman. Possessing desirable qualities that reach deeper than physical appearance, this nameless woman demonstrates remarkable ability to accept her barren plight, and to acknowledge removal of that reproach. Eager to incorporate her husband into her special moments, she does not hesitate to rebuke him when occasion requires it. Neither stunned by incredible tidings nor frightened in divine presence, she represents the noblest kind of Israelite mother. But she symbolizes more than a mother; for some time she was someone's available daughter, whom Manoah chose for her remarkable virtues. She thus stands for the ideal Israelite wife.

The other three units juxtapose non-Israelite women over against Manoah's wife. They represent three kinds of alliances: the power of physical attraction, physical lust, and unreciprocated love. The first episode (14:1—15:20) presents another impressive woman, who naturally captures Samson's affection. In so doing she precipitates a crisis in his relations with his parents, bringing to focus a conflict between parental devotion and physical desire, love and pleasure. The choice of a foreigner only complicates matters; such a bond inevitably leads to heartbreak and dismay. The second episode (16:1–3) presents an entirely different kind of eros, one based on physical gratification alone. Whereas the first story highlights the dangers of involvement with a lovely foreigner, the second points out certain repercussions of a one night stand. It suggests that nameless cavorting with harlots possesses its difficulties too, especially when those women of the night do not belong to Israelite fathers. The final episode (16:4–31) introduces another kind of relationship, one based on unrequited love.

Although the text remains silent about Delilah's ancestry, it gives the impression that she belongs on the other side of the ethnological fence from Samson.[5] Her ability to communicate with Samson hardly requires us to view her as an Israelite. Samson seems capable of conversing with the Timnite, and Philistines talk freely with people from Judah. The saga records no conversation between Samson and the harlot, so we shall gain little from an appeal to that incident. It suffices that the narrator assumed that linguistic differences between Israelite and Philistine posed no serious problem.

Whether Israelite or Philistine, Delilah capitalizes on Samson's confession of love and penetrates his innermost secret. Too late, Samson learns that whoever warms himself by the enemy fire gets burnt in the end.[6] If the great Samson could not withstand pressure from these erotic relationships, the saga implies, how can ordinary Israelites survive such alliances?

With this purpose in mind, let us examine the four episodes to see how they contribute to delineating four kinds of relationships with women. We turn first to the combined birth narrative and recognition story, which consists of five scenes (13:1–5, 6–7, 8–18, 19–23, 24–25).

The Ideal Israelite Wife

The story opens with a brief description of Israel's apostasy that provoked the Lord's anger and subjected Israelites to Philistines. The formulaic language belongs to the Deuteronomistic editor, who judged Israel's history in terms of faithfulness to the Lord. How did he determine whether a generation measured up to God's demands? Israel's kings were judged on the basis of their implementation of exclusive worship at Jerusalem. Premonarchic Israel seems to have been judged by the purity of her worship. Apostasy to Baal constitutes the evil for which Philistines as the Lord's agents punished her. The editor assumes that Israel imbibed a poison that infiltrated her system, governing all actions and spurring her on to faithlessness.

Having supplied a framework for the narrative, the editor permits the story to stand as is. It opens with a familiar formula typical of folklore, Israel's equivalent to "Once upon a time." "There was a man from Zorah belonging to the Danite clan." Those familiar with traditions about this clan would probably not have expected anything extraordinary from such a lineage. For had not Dan found it impossible to maintain territory in the southern region? Periodic attack from Philistines finally compelled the Danites to look for safer residence; they moved as far north of the Philistines as possible.

Danites may have defended their decision to move as prudence, but others identified the change in territory as cowardice. Another tradition, preserved as a sequel to the Samson saga, describes these Danites as courageous—when they outnumbered their enemy six hundred to one. The Danites knew no law other than self-interest, and readily stole to assure their prosperity. Moreover, they slaughtered a city, Laish, and made it their own (Judges 18). The description of Laish's inhabitants as people who dwelt alone at peace contains an implicit attack on the Danites, who saw this fact as particularly favorable to their chances of defeating Laish without retaliation from neighboring peoples.

Typically, the man is introduced first. His wife follows. Manoah, like his ancestors, had his problems. His unnamed wife was barren. Those who had expected little from a Danite smile knowingly. Manoah's wife bore reproach because Danites hardly conform to Israel's standards of morality and courage. The hendiadys (two words expressing one meaning, like "assault and battery") emphasizes her plight. She was barren and had not given birth.

Without the slightest fanfare, an angel of Yahweh appeared and announced a reversal of her fortune. Suddenly, expectations change. Perhaps, after all, a Danite can display characteristics worthy of emulation. No word is spoken about reasons for the woman's barrenness; the slightest accusation is lacking. Nor do we hear anything about her agony—or even whether she prayed for God's assistance. Her role is entirely passive. She becomes a symbol of God's watchful eye during human distress. Others may think God has abandoned her, but the angel proclaims another message. We may speculate about her

reaction to barrenness, but we cannot say she resembles Rachel
who complained bitterly to her husband or Hannah who begged
God for a son. Instead, like Sarah she simply heard the messenger's annunciation, but unlike her earlier ancestor, Manoah's
wife believed the good tidings.

The angel appeared to the woman. Strangely, here she is not
identified as Manoah's wife. We may pause long enough to
reflect on the anonymity of this woman. Apparently, the tradition did not record a name for her. The narrator could certainly
have done so, if he had wished. Perhaps the absence of a name
here and in the following two episodes is intentional. It strikes
one as ironical that a nameless person can be trustworthy,
whereas a person whose name we know, Delilah, proved false.
In the case of the lovely Timnite, no name is given; but she
betrayed Samson from necessity. A still better explanation for
the lack of a name concerns the quest for the angel's name.
Since the woman is nameless, in terms of the story, she does not
probe the angel's identity. This woman remains content with
an impersonal relationship. Given such wondrous news, why   ?
ask questions?

The initial words of the angel seem cruel in the extreme. A
stranger approached the poor woman with the greeting, "Look
here, woman, you are barren and have not given birth." The
conclusion makes amends, for he told her everything she ever
wanted to know and more: "You shall conceive and give birth
to a son." The angel proceeded to instruct the woman in regard
to her diet during pregnancy. She must avoid alcoholic beverages, and must not eat anything unclean.

Not a single word of joy or gratitude falls from the woman's
lips. Nor do we hear an implicit rebuke, "It's about time."
Instead, we encounter a duplication of the original message,
with an important specification. It answers the unspoken question, "Why should I watch my diet so carefully?" The lad will
be a Nazirite to the Lord from birth. Now we hear a further
directive: A razor must not go up on his head. And the lad's role
becomes clear: He will begin to deliver Israel from the hand of
the Philistines.

One has the suspicion that this replication of the original

message derives from another hand than the author of the
saga. This impression rests on the fact that Samson's Nazirite
status hardly functions in the story. In addition, the repetition
of the angel's greeting scarcely contributes to the story, but
functions to connect primary and secondary material. Further
evidence comes from the grand charge bestowed upon the un-
born lad. The saga contains no single act of Samson that accords with this majestic calling. Instead of beginning Israel's
deliverance, Samson carries on a personal feud with his enemies, who just happen to be Israel's antagonists. In any event,
this brief note affirms God's concern for personal and national
interests. He delivers a barren woman from her agony, and at
the same time provides a means of saving all Israel.

In the second scene the woman told her husband everything
about the memorable encounter with God's emissary, whom
she describes as a man of God with an awesome countenance.
The woman's report emphasizes her proper conduct; she did
not invite ridicule by conversing freely with a stranger on a
name basis.[7] She protects herself by alerting her husband to
the wondrous demeanor of the man of God. Intuitively, she had
recognized him as God's angel; but her words to Manoah couch
that recognition in cautious similitude. The man was *like* an
angel of God, exceedingly awesome in appearance. Therefore,
she reports, she had kept her distance from him, and Manoah
had no cause for concern. This woman does not merely repeat
the angel's message. Just as she had interpreted his countenance as an indication of his origin, she added an important
phrase to the angel's words. The lad will be a Nazirite of
Yahweh from birth *until the day of his death.* Like Eve, she
exercises remarkable freedom in interpreting the sense of a
directive from the Lord. To God's prohibition, "You must not
eat from the tree in the midst of the garden," Eve added, perhaps for her own protection, "You must not even touch it." So
Manoah's wife tempers jubilance with a hint of things to come.

The third scene consists of Manoah's attempt to enter the
limelight. Eager to meet this man of God and to inquire about
further instructions, Manoah prayed that the messenger would

appear to him and his wife. Did Manoah not trust his wife's account of what had transpired? Did he wish corroboration by his own eyes and ears of what his wife's body would soon proclaim dramatically? Since God heard his prayer and sent his angel again, perhaps we should not view the narrative as reflecting badly on his character. On the other hand, the angel's stern words to Manoah add nothing except a reminder that he should listen to his wife more carefully. The narrative reflects negatively on Manoah,[8] it follows, but minimally so.

The angel appeared to the woman who was sitting in the field. This location hardly reads like the usual place for such confrontation. Perhaps the place anticipates Samson's subsequent action in the enemy's field. Knowing her husband's eagerness to meet the man of God, the woman hastens to her husband with her news that his prayer has been answered. Surprisingly, the verb shifts at this point; Manoah followed his wife to the scene of the meeting. Nothing is said of his running, in contrast to his wife's hasty journey.

Manoah's greeting approaches rudeness: "Are you the man who spoke with this woman?" Is this an example of the adage, "Fools rush in where angels fear to tread"? Why does Manoah not identify his wife? Surely she deserves something better than "this woman." He probes for more information: When your words materialize, what will the lad be like? Manoah asked that life's surprises be taken away. He wants to know what will characterize the lad, both in his way of life and his accomplishments. The angel merely reinforced his earlier instructions, urging Manoah to see that the wife abides by them.

Not content with the encounter to this point, Manoah attempted to prolong the conversation by suggesting that he prepare a feast in the man's honor. Like Abraham who had provided a sumptuous meal for God and his angels who came with the news that Sarah would give birth to a son, Manoah wished to pay homage to his guest. The messenger declined the offer of food, and suggested an offering to God instead. Persistent to the end, Manoah played his trump card. He asked the man's name so he could honor him at a later date when the son was born. Refusing to surrender his identity casually, the angel offered a clue to his name.[9] Seizing that clue, Manoah demonstrated his worth by his actions at a sacred altar.

The fourth scene takes place around holy fire. Since the angel had chosen to make his name known by a veiled reference to "wonder," Manoah showed that he was capable of a similar communication of his own identity. The angel suggested that Manoah offer up a burnt offering to God. Manoah combined a cereal offering with it. Now the word for cereal offering, *minchah*, resembles Manoah's own name, and constitutes his declaration that he understood the angel's hint. The one to whom Manoah dedicated the offerings confirms the view that he clearly grasped the angel's clue, for he gave them to *Yahweh*, the one performing wonders. Twice the narrator tells us that husband and wife watched the altar, presumably to determine whether or not the Lord accepted the sacrifice.

What the two beheld left no doubt in their minds about God's willingness to accept their offerings. As the flames climbed upward from the rock, the angel slowly ascended in the midst of the fire. Overcome by awe, both fell to the ground. Reflection upon the absence of the angel convinced Manoah that the messenger had indeed been Yahweh's angel. Why the silence about Manoah's wife? Surely the narrator implies that she had known the angel's identity from the beginning.

Manoah's response to the angel's departure, wholly natural, acknowledges finitude in the presence of infinity. Appropriately, a temporal reference occurs to pave the way for his expression of dread. Inasmuch as the Lord's angel did not *again* appear to Manoah and his wife, Manoah knew that the messenger was indeed Yahweh's. Therefore, Manoah believed he and his wife were doomed, having looked upon God. Forgetting the joyous announcement that his wife would bear a son who would begin to deliver Israel, Manoah conceded his creaturehood. His wife acknowledged her temporality, too, in her own way. After all, she joined Manoah in falling to the ground. But no power in heaven or upon earth could compel her to abandon a newfound hope. So she reasoned that those wondrous events could

only come from God. It followed that the one who had proclaimed this joyous news would not have shown them such
things or accepted their offerings if he intended to slay them.
Therefore, Manoah's wife gently rebuked her husband, and
confessed her abiding confidence in him who had removed her
reproach.[10]

The last scene reports that event first proclaimed by the
man of God, and afterwards believed by wife and husband.
The woman who deigned to converse with an angel, to look
on God and his angel with full trust, and to scold her husband gave birth to a son and named him Samson. Her
choice of a name reflects abiding faith in the angel's announcement of the lad's role as deliverer. She bestows such
confidence on her son, naming him "little sun" or "solar
one." A final word concludes the first episode: The lad grew
and the Lord blessed him. At Mahaneh-dan, between Zorah
and Eshtaol, the Lord's spirit began to stir him. We are not
to think, therefore, that all Samson's deeds have entered the
saga.

Marriage Based on Physical Beauty

The second episode also consists of five scenes: (1) 14:1–9,
preparations for a wedding; (2) 14:10–20, wedding festivities; (3)
15:1–8, attempt at reconciliation; (4) 15:9–17, hand to hand
combat; and (5) 15:18–19, request for help. In addition, two
editorial remarks have been interspersed within the account
(14:4; 15:20). The story illustrates the danger inherent in a
relationship with a foreign woman whose chief asset is ravishing beauty.

The initial scene describes Samson's chance meeting of a
lovely Timnite and his arrangements to marry her. On an
excursion to nearby Timnah, Samson saw a woman who caught
his eye. Returning to his home at Zorah, he told his father
about her and suggested that he arrange a marriage for them.
Samson's father objected at first, but finally acquiesced. Samson returned to Timnah to confirm his intentions with the
woman; en route he slew a lion with his bare hands. The two

young people met, conversed, and decided to join hands in mat-
rimony. On his way to the wedding, Samson stopped long
enough to examine the carcass of the lion, and to his astonishment, found bees and honey inside it. Scooping some up with
his hand, Samson went his way eating honey, and he also
shared it with his parents.

The object of Samson's desire is called "a woman in Timnah
from the daughters of the Philistines." Interestingly, she does
not receive the customary title of honor, "maiden," or the alternative characterization, "a maiden, a virgin." Such deficiency
hardly justifies viewing the Timnite as a woman of questionable morals; the form of the description does not cast aspersion
on the woman's character at all.[11]

Samson's conduct suggests that he wanted to erase distinc-
tions between Danite and Philistine. His views in this area
clashed sharply with his father's, the guardian of endogamy.
Manoah's response to Samson's request that he arrange a marriage with the Timnite bristles with shock and dismay: "Is
there not a woman among the daughters of your brothers and
among all my people that you must take a wife from the uncircumcised Philistines?" Samson put an end to the discussion
with a quasi-command: "Get her for me, for she is right in my
eyes."

An editor has inserted an explanation at this point in the
story (14:4), to the effect that Samson's parents did not realize
that the Lord had prompted Samson's actions, since he wanted
an occasion with the Philistines who ruled at that time over
Israel. We may pause, therefore, to discuss the fundamental
issue posed by Samson's request. That issue concerns marriage
with a foreigner (exogamy).

The traditions of Israel maintain constant tension between
endogamy and exogamy.[12] On the one hand, certain notable
figures choose wives from neighboring peoples without censure.
On the other, sharp polemic occurs where certain alliances
with non-Israelites take place. We have already alluded to
Abraham's express anxiety that Isaac might choose a wife from
local women. Moses and David hardly give the matter of ex-

ogamy a moment's reflection. Each takes wives freely from non-Israelites, and such action evokes no expression of raised eyebrows on that account.

The two competing views, endogamy and exogamy, have generated paradigmatic literary units. In defense of marriage outside the ranks of Israelites, the Book of Ruth contends that the king after God's own heart traces his ancestry to a mixed marriage, that between Boaz and Ruth, a Moabite. The incident of Baal-Peor, recorded in Numbers 25:1–18, presents an opposing viewpoint. While at Shittim, Israelites contracted marriages with Midianite women, and joined them in worshipping Baal of Peor. Yahweh commanded that the offenders be slain, and it was done. A certain Israelite brought a Midianite wife into his tent in open defiance of Moses and his understanding of God's will. A quick-acting Phinehas, son of Eleazar son of Aaron the priest, grabbed a spear, entered the offender's tent, and pierced both husband and wife through, presumably during coitus. Thus Yahweh's wrath abated; nevertheless, his plague slew twenty-four thousand Israelites. As reward, Yahweh gave Phinehas a covenant of perpetual priesthood. The anecdote goes on to specify the actual names of the unfortunate pair: Zimri and Cozbi. Furthermore, it gives divine sanction to harassment of the Midianites who provided occasion for the terrible offense in Yahweh's eyes.

These opposing viewpoints continued to surface throughout Israel's history. They became intensified during special threats to the people's existence, for example, during the period of the restoration under Nehemiah and Ezra. Spokesmen for endogamy, these political and spiritual leaders respectively inaugurated harsh measures to assure genealogical purity. Surprisingly, those responsible for formulating a biblical canon demonstrated considerably more open-mindedness on this matter, incorporating the Book of Jonah into the collection of the Prophets. In this little book, nothing explicit is said about marriage with foreigners, but such positive treatment of non-Israelites as is found in the book of Jonah naturally implies openness to exogamy.

Opposition to intermarriage with foreigners arose from a valid intuition, the desire to assure integrity of worship. An atypical characteristic of Yahweh, his insistence upon sole allegiance, left no room for compromise. Whereas other deities accomodated divided commitment, Yahweh demanded that his worshippers choose between him and opposing claims of loyalty. The person who desired to serve Yahweh and Baal, though persistently present in Israel, was considered an abomination to Yahweh. The survival of Yahwism depended, it was again and again claimed, upon the eradication of the Canaanites whose rival religion threatened Yahwistic purity.

This view of non-Israelites affected judgments made about Israel's greatest heroes. King Solomon's grandeur became tarnished in the eyes of his "historian" because of that monarch's lax policy concerning exogamy. Marriages contracted with foreigners endangered Yahwism, especially when the foreign wife claimed Pharaoh as father. Yoked to such women, Solomon in all his wisdom and glory could not maintain the integrity of his faith, in this "historian's" opinion (1 Kings 11:1–8).

The arch-villian of Israel's kings, Ahab, owes his notoriety to a wedding with the daughter of Tyre's king. This infamous Jezebel introduced alien worship into the center of Israel's daily life, the capital. Moreover, her ruthless disdain for ethical standards sacred to Yahweh spelled disaster for anyone who stood up for traditional values, as Naboth discovered too late (1 Kings 21). The mere news that Jezebel had sworn to kill Elijah sent him on a journey into self-pity and gave rise to his death wish. And that news came on the heels of Elijah's awesome victory over Baalistic prophets on Mount Carmel. It arrived, that is, at the moment of the faithful prophet's greatest triumph (1 Kings 18:17—19:4).

This polemic against foreign women, which we have discovered in many different literary and historical contexts, even occurs in wisdom literature,[13] where one would not expect to find it because of the international flavor of sapiential thought. In Proverbs, warning against the foreign woman constitutes a major motif, all the more astonishing since extended themes do not generally appear in proverbial texts. In this regard, Sirach varies earlier instructions considerably, for Jesus ben Sira shows a distinct fondness for extensive treatments of certain themes.[14]

Opinions differ about the identity of the foreign woman in Proverbs. In some cases she seems to be an Israelite, and "foreign" implies breach of the marriage bond. Other texts are best understood in the light of the cultic situation in Mesopotamia. In these, the foreign woman belongs to the cadre of sacred prostitutes who offer their services at official sanctuaries. Still other passages probably refer to non-Israelites, without any cultic overtones. These foreign women posed a serious threat to sexual morals; when young men surrendered to their enticements, they invited death at the hands of an irate husband who would stop at nothing to get back at one who had cuckolded him. In view of such a woman's power over potential sages, and ordinary Israelites as well, the move to personify her as Dame Folly[15] seems appropriate. Whoever is wise will choose Dame Wisdom as his bride.

How can we explain Israel's constant infatuation with foreign women? One explanation certainly rests in the cultural advantages of non-Israelites, particularly those residing in great cultural centers, but to some degree possessed by ordinary Canaanites. Superiority in cosmetic aids, clothing and utensils of all sorts certainly belonged to early Canaanites, if archaeological interpretations for this period are reliable.[16] Furthermore, Canaanite women possessed the advantage of "mystery," since they were relatively unknown. Foreign women always had different features and behavior patterns that intrigued and lured men away from the familiar women they thought they knew so well. In addition, foreigners who lived in Israel's midst exercised less restraint, especially since their religion encouraged sexual license. In short, foreign women had the distinct advantage of the "unknown" and the lure of the "uninhibited."

Like so many before and after him, Samson fell prey to these enticements. It mattered little to him that the Timnite belonged to the uncircumcised Philistines, to use Manoah's contemptuous expression. In Samson's eyes she was right. Older folks could argue themselves hoarse in defense of endogamy, for all he cared; but Samson knew what his senses wanted, and would obtain her at any price.

The first coin that Samson gave up was harmony within his father's household. With his bold demand, "Get her for me, for she is right in my eyes," Samson threw off paternal authority once and for all time. Manoah's reaction was dictated by the circumstances, resulting in compromise in the face of a defiant son whose strength was matchless. The narrative remains silent about the aged father's thoughts as he made journeys southward to secure the Timnite woman for his son, but one can rightly imagine that each step was taken with immense pain.[17]

It may be that the rift between Samson and his parents was so great that Manoah arranged a special kind of marriage for Samson and the woman, a union called *tsadiqah* marriage. In this arrangement the wife remains with her family, and the husband abandons his parents to live with his wife, or he visits her periodically. Such a marriage assured a woman of protection by her household, and was particularly advantageous to herdsmen who followed their cattle and sheep in search of pasturage.

Remnants of the *tsadiqah* marriage survive in biblical narratives. The observation in Genesis 2:24 that endeavors to explain the erotic impulse in a manner similar to Plato's Androgenes myth reflects such a relationship between a husband, who leaves his father and mother, and a wife. Specific examples of *tsadiqah* marriage have survived, if at all, only in the stories of Jacob and Moses, both of whom lived with their in-laws. Perhaps these two unusual marriages merely reflect the special circumstances of the patriarch and Israel's great leader, both of whom had burned their bridges and could hardly return to their homes with newfound brides.

An argument in favor of the theory of a *tsadiqah* marriage behind Samson's journey to Timnah, the actual site of the wedding feast, may have been generated by the necessities of the plot. At Timnah the presence and behavior of the thirty Philistine groomsmen was entirely appropriate to the circumstances. Had the wedding feast taken place in Zorah, these foreigners could hardly have flaunted their power over life and limb.

In short, we cannot determine whether Samson's wedding belongs to a *tsadiqah* marriage or not. About one thing, however, the text leaves no doubt. The Lord stood behind everything Samson did, although neither the hungry lover nor his parents grasped the significance of the infatuation. This little bit of information, concealed from the actors, gives those viewing the action from afar special advantage. Such attempts to provide essential data give the audience or the reader a feeling of omniscience. Spectators know something that even the main characters do not. The literary device functions to relieve tension in dramatic episodes; a particularly powerful example occurs within Genesis 22,[18] where the reader is told that God's demand that Abraham sacrifice his only son, Isaac, constitutes a test. By this bit of information we know the outcome from the beginning, while Abraham remains in darkness until the very end (cf. also the prologue to Job).

This brief remark identifies Philistines as *Yahweh's* enemies, and portrays Israel's God as one bent on provoking the foe by any possible means. Such a reading of current events derives from a theocentric view of reality; whatever happened reflected divine purpose, whether the instruments of that will perceived his hand behind their actions or not.

The tendency to assume that God's heroes understood the deeper reasons for their behavior prompted Milton to depict Samson as one who correctly perceived divine purpose behind his stirrings of passion.

> . . . They knew not
> That what I motion'd was of God; I knew
> From intimate impulse, and therefore urged
> The Marriage on; (221–224).[19]

Samson thus loses something that belongs to the essence of the biblical narrative, his credibility.

Having assured the audience that Samson's actions cannot

abort, the narrator has him and his parents journey to Timnah
to arrange a wedding. En route a lion confronts Samson, who
happens to be alone at the time. How should we interpret this
incident?

In some traditions lions serve to punish violators of the
covenant or disobedient men of God.[20] Did the Nazirite venture
too close to vineyards, thus necessitating a warning from God?
If the Nazirite vow belonged to the center of the story of Samson, rather than on the periphery, such a view would offer an
attractive explanation for the incident. Still, one would have to
explain Samson's ability to overcome a lion sent by God, which
would take some doing. Certainly the lions in God's service
elsewhere encounter no real opposition to their purposes. In all
probability the incident of the lion has no deeper meaning than
that provided in Samson's later riddle.

Needless to say, the lovely Timnite pleased Samson when
they came together to discuss marriage. After Samson's break
with his parents, he could hardly reverse his opinion of the
Timnite. Another journey to Zorah, and still another trip back
to Timnah stood between them and marital bliss. On the latter
trek, Samson satisfied his curiosity about the carcass of the lion
and discovered a remarkable bonus.

Perhaps a word is in order about Samson's fascination for
animal carcasses, particularly in light of the claim that he
would be a Nazirite to God. What compelled Samson to gather
honey from the carcass and to eat his fill? And at a later time,
what explains his readiness to grab a fresh jawbone of an ass
as a weapon against the onrushing Philistines? Surely Samson
did not look upon himself as one who had to avoid anything
unclean.

The second scene describes events surrounding the week-
long wedding festival that took place in the bride's home. We
do not know why Samson's companions belonged to the Philistine camp; textual variants suggest two possible reasons, both
based on similar Hebrew words. The Massoretic Text reads
"when they saw him," but the Greek "because they feared
him" suggests another reason for the selection of Philistine

companions. One could view the Greek rendering as a fortunate error in translation,[21] one that draws out the actual result of their seeing Samson. One look at this mighty man suggested caution, and dictated the choice of thirty Philistines to assure everyone's safety. After all, the local Timnites had every right to be suspicious of Samson's intentions, since he belonged to the Danite clan.

Undaunted by the presence of thirty Philistines, Samson quickly challenged them to a contest of wits. Since, according to the Book of Job, even God could not turn his back on a wager, these thirty Philistines enthusiastically seized the occasion to demonstrate their superiority over the foreigner who had already invaded their ranks and grabbed up their loveliest prize. The staggering odds, thirty to one, seem not to have disturbed Samson, who knew that the key to his riddle nestled snugly in his own thoughts.

We shall forego discussion of Samson's riddle until the following chapter. For now, we shall simply say that Samson's confidence in his ability to retain his secret was grossly misplaced. Eventually, he revealed the decisive clue to the interpretation of his riddle, opened his heart, that is, to a tearful bride. Little did he realize that the woman to whom he had entrusted his soul would betray him to the thirty companions.

Samson's reaction to the Philistine's successful unraveling of his riddle hardly serves as an example of gracious losing. Bitter over his loss of face in the eyes of all the wedding guests, and angry that his own wife had betrayed him, Samson stormed out of the house in a fit of passion equal to his passionate anticipation of entering the bridal chamber. His fury led him to Askelon, one of the five chief cities of Philistia, where he fell upon thirty men and stripped them of their garments. With this bloody spoil, Samson paid his debt to the thirty companions. The irony in this payment escaped the ken of these men whose preoccupation with their own little victory made them oblivious to a minor catastrophe that had struck one of the cities of the Philistine pentapolis.

Having covered his wager with someone else's coverings,

Samson returned to his father's house in utter bitterness. The narrator spares us any word about Manoah's "I told you so," nor does he permit us entry into Samson's private thoughts after this initial disappointment at love. Milton could not resist the temptation to supply the former; the old Manoah reminds the enslaved son:

> I cannot praise your marriage choises, Son,
> Rather approve them not; but thou didst plead
> Divine impulsion prompting how thou might'st
> Find some occasion to infest our Foes (420–423).

The narrator does, however, provide one interesting detail which Samson's hasty departure precipitated. His wife was given to his "best man." Once again we possess vital information that Samson will learn as the story unfolds.

The third scene records Samson's bid at reconciliation with his wife, and the resulting events. Time's healing power worked wonders, and Samson remembered the beautiful Timnite whom he had shamed by word and deed. Samson's memory overwhelmed him during the joyous harvest festival, and he determined to visit his wife. Taking along a kid, presumably as a reconciliation gift to the injured bride, Samson arrived at her home and declared his intention to enter his wife's chamber.

This time someone else stood between Samson and his bride. The father-in-law refused Samson entrance into the woman's room. The mighty Samson, who had walked roughshod over his own father's wishes, submitted docilely to this man. Apparently, tradition could not bear to conceive of Samson as a home-breaker. Cavorting with harlots was one thing, but breaking up another person's marriage was beneath Samson's dignity. So Samson in all his strength stood outside his wife's chamber.[22]

The conversation between Samson and the father-in-law plumbs the depths of despair. Self-justification characterizes the father's speech. At the same time, he points an accusing finger at Samson, whose actions convinced the father that Samson hated his bride. Samson's disparaging remark about his heifer, and his hasty departure in anger convinced the father that the marriage had been annulled. That is the force of his self-quotation: "I thought, 'He really hates her.' " The father thus defended his transfer of the bride to another person, since Samson had behaved publicly like one who seeks a divorce.[23]

But the father did not stop with accusation. Recognizing his own culpability, he offered Samson a substitute bride. Fortunately, the wife had a little sister who was better than she; Samson could thus come out ahead in the deal. Samson, who had already shown his own father that no one else would choose his bride for him, understood the insult concealed within the offer, and refused it. After all, if the sister had been so ravishing, Samson's original choice becomes a questionable one.

For a third time Samson left the Timnite's house in anger. This time he decided to perpetrate some mischief on the Philistines who had caused all the trouble at Timnah. Catching three hundred foxes, or jackals, Samson ignited torches between each pair of tails and turned the animals loose in Philistine grain fields and olive orchards. The Philistines inquired about the guilty culprit, and discovered both his name and the reason for his actions. We must not ask how the unnamed informants happened upon this valuable knowledge; in saga such things simply occur, for the plot dictates them.

The incident of the foxes belongs to a common store of mythological traditions in the ancient world. Ovid informs us that foxes with lighted tails were turned loose in the Circus during Cerealia in April, presumably to commemorate a calamity caused by a youngster's igniting tails of some foxes. Alternatively, the incident may reflect an old practice of warding off blight and mildew by using heat generated by lively animals. In any case, the story represents Samson as the perpetrator of considerable destruction.

We ought to recognize the irony within the account of the Philistines' quick revenge. They burned the Timnite family; Samson's conduct precipitated strife within the ranks of the enemy. Whereas propriety had prevented Samson from storming the Timnite's household, his enemies accomplished that feat for him.

Samson saw nothing humorous in the flaming house. Although we hear nothing about his thoughts concerning the awful fate of his wife, we are informed of his revulsion at such an enemy. This must certainly be the meaning of his determination to get revenge and to quit afterwards. If the Philistines behave so cruelly, he will break off all dealings with them. So Samson satisfied his thirst for revenge, and afterwards fled to a refuge.

Samson's desire to isolate himself from cruel reality, like his wish to enjoy marital pleasure, was frustrated. The fourth scene describes Samson's re-entry into the heat of battle. Fraternal rivalry now invaded Israel's ranks, just as it had surfaced in Philistia. Philistine encampment within Judah's territory evoked terror in the hearts of subject peoples. Eager to ascertain the cause of this invasion, they inquired of the Philistines and learned that Samson had brought on this attack. Instead of rushing to defend their brother, the men of Judah decided to save their necks by handing Samson over to the enemy. After all, they reasoned, the Philistines' claim is just.

Three thousand brave men sauntered to Samson's hiding place, forgetting all claims a Danite might make on Judahites. Having become accustomed to foreign rule, they chided Samson for ignoring political reality. Milton saw their awful bondage with exceptional clarity.

> But what more oft, in Nations grown corrupt,
> And by their vices brought to servitude,
> Then to love Bondage more than Liberty . . .
> Bondage with ease than strenuous liberty; . . . (268–271).

Although these men counted ties of brotherhood refuse, Samson refused to follow them in self-deceit and self-interest. Instead he devised a means of preventing a slaughter of his own people. By obtaining an oath from the men of Judah that they would not harm him, Samson made certain that he would not have to kill members of a brother tribe. He then allowed the self-seeking Judahites to tie him up with two fresh ropes, and accompanied them to meet the Philistines.

We marvel at the negative portrayal of men of Judah, who receive a much better press elsewhere in Israel's traditions. Even the story of Judah and Tamar, though distinctly unfavorable to Judah, recognizes in him a sense of fair play (Genesis 38). Judah admitted that Tamar had acted more justly than he, for she had merely obtained the child that rightly belonged to a widow whose husband left her no progeny. Furthermore, Judah behaved respectably in one version of the Joseph story, when all his brothers sought Joseph's life.

In all probability the Samson saga reflects Danite tradition, whereas these other stories derive from the tradition of Judah. The irony of the Samson story being discussed would hardly have escaped later audiences, who remembered that a member of the tribe of Judah finally removed the Philistine threat to survival. Capitalizing on Saul's victories over Israel's enemy rulers, the great David put an end to Philistine hegemony. What the three thousand men of Judah feared to do, and what Samson only began to carry out, David accomplished with crushing finality.

These obliging Judahites led the securely-tied Samson toward the waiting Philistines, who rushed to seize their prey. Yahweh's spirit chose that moment to rush upon Samson, who threw off the ropes and rose to the occasion. A thousand Philistines fell before Samson's rude weapon. Curiously, the Judahites did not rally behind Samson to throw off the yoke of foreign rule. Milton has Samson lament the failure of his brethren:

> Had *Judah* that day join'd, or one whole Tribe,
> They had by this possess'd, the Towers of *Gath*,
> And lorded over them whom now they serve; . . . (265–267)

Samson, on the other hand, thought only of the glorious victory he had achieved, and immortalized that deed in song. He spared the cowardly Judahites any mention in this victory chant, and concentrated solely on the unusual weapon, an ass's jawbone.

The final scene in this second episode of the Samson saga

consists of an appendix. Such vigorous activity must have ex-
hausted Samson. Thirsty, and fearing death from its effects,
Samson prayed as effectively as he had earlier waged battle.
Unlike the Judahites, God came to Samson's assistance.

We pause at the close of our discussion of the second episode
to comment on the remarkable ending. At Samson's greatest
moment we have our attention diverted to another actor in the
story. A similar phenomenon transpired in the first episode.
There the story culminates in awesome theophany and a reference to divine blessing. Both episodes praise Samson in
extreme language, whether predictive or reportive. But each
episode points to a deeper reality that makes Samson's exploits
possible. This living God blessed the lad and hearkened to the
thirsty warrior.

Physical Lust Outside Marriage

The brief third episode presents yet another kind of relationship between an Israelite and a foreign woman. Here Samson drowned his memories in the arms of a harlot. Chafing from
the searing rebuke by the lovely Timnite that he did not love
her, Samson sought a relationship where love played no role.
Thus forever freed from the necessity of proving his love, Samson spent his passion safely. It did not take him long, however,
to realize that his late wife's charge of lovelessness must be
dealt with openly once and for all. To do that, and consequently
to neutralize the memory of his first love affair, Samson must
forsake luxuriating in the arms of some nameless harlot and
surrender to love's summons. This inevitable self-justification
will lead him once again into the inner chamber of a Philistine
woman.

The brevity of the interlude with a harlot in Gaza poses
special hazards. The natural tendency to rush ahead in the
story to discover Samson's success in demonstrating his capacity for love must be combatted. And the delicacy of the subject
matter puts considerable strain on our sense of what is proper;
for the ancient narrator, no such problem existed. Harlots
played a vital role in his society, and Samson, who had been
robbed of a wife, sought to take advantage of this vitality.

A single word characterizes this object of Samson's amorous attention. That word, harlot, suffices. We are not told whether she was beautiful, or articulate, or even how successfully she performed her vocation. Perhaps we may infer, as the Israelite audience surely must have, that she wasn't very good as a harlot. In any case, she failed to captivate Samson for a full night. Samson's restlessness in the arms of the Timnite seems to have arisen from her copious tears, and the same illness will strike him in Delilah's arms because of her constant banter. But this harlot cannot hold Samson by any means; after a few hours he gets up and abandons her bed.

The reader can barely resist a temptation to repeat an earlier remark supplied by the editor. Samson saw a harlot at Gaza and went in to her, *as was his custom.* The narrator does supply some important data that Samson must have intuited. Somehow news of Samson's presence in the city spread rapidly, and brave men took up strategic positions surrounding his only route of escape. While Samson's attentions are focused elsewhere, our eyes politely steal away to ominous events on the outside. Confident that their ambush would prove effective against a notorious foe, these Gazites postponed action until the light of day. We should catch the coarse humor behind their strategy. After a night of love's labor, Samson would scarcely be in a position to withstand their attack.[24] Had not even the mighty Enkidu experienced slackened pace after his record-setting inauguration into the pleasures offered by a harlot lass?

Samson proved that even the best laid plans can go wrong. Hardly weakened by his expenditure of energy, he arose and walked away with the gate to the city, leaving Gaza exposed to danger from attack. Depositing the gate and its posts far enough away so that Gazites could not retrieve them, Samson demonstrated his mastery over the men of Gaza. But what will he do when his enemy is a woman?

Unreciprocated Love

The final episode in the Samson saga consists of three scenes: (1) the discovery of Samson's secret (16:5–20); (2) his downfall (16:21–22); and (3) Samson's revenge (16:23–30). A

brief introduction (16:4) and conclusion (16:31) set off this material. The episode dramatizes the tragic effects of loving a
woman who does not respond in kind. Ironically, Samson's
successful refutation of the Timnite's charge of lovelessness
brings his downfall.

The introductory comment differs in every respect from the
formula describing Samson's discovery of his two earlier
women. A temporal adverb, "afterwards," prevents the isolat-
ing of this story from previous ones. It brings the various episodes together in more than temporal fashion, for the brief
glance backwards functions to contrast the different kinds of
amorous adventures. The striking introductory observation
differs in two other fundamentals: It labels the bond that drew
Samson to the woman "love," and it bestows a name upon the
fortunate female. This story shifts from an account of marriage
entered upon because of a woman's pleasing appearance, and
from the pleasures obtained in a harlot's bed. It approaches the
sublime: Samson actually loves a woman. The woman's name,
Delilah, is an appropriate one from Samson's perspective. Its
meaning approximates "darling."

Such names occur elsewhere in the Hebrew Scriptures, specifically in the book of Job. The epilogue leaves Job's new seven
sons nameless, but gives his three daughters' names. Each belongs to the realm of folklore: Dove, Cinnamon, and Horn of
Eye Paint. Just as we do not know whether the biblical Job and
his children are viewed as Israelites, so we are not given Delilah's nationality. If habit means anything, one should assume
that she belongs to the camp of the Philistines. Twice already
Samson has fallen for a non-Israelite, and nothing suggests any
variation in this pattern.

The opening scene constitutes Hebrew narrative art at its
finest. It makes copious use of refrains and dialogue, sustaining
suspense to the last. Even when the vocabulary becomes expansive, it derives from the psychological state of the speaker. For
instance, the Philistines' verbosity suggests agitation of spirit
and general fright at the very thought of tangling with the
mighty Samson.

This expression of their wishes omits an important verb. Nowhere in all the verbiage did the Philistine lords mention *slaying* Samson. Instead, they instructed Delilah to find out "in what way his strength is great, and in what way we may overpower him and bind him, to afflict him." On the basis of this language, and subsequent narrative material, we must conclude that the Philistines wanted to expose Samson to painful and humiliating bondage over a period of time. In this way they would savor the taste of victory for years to come.

These Philistine lords offer a bribe instead of wielding a threat like their thirty counterparts, but their language overlaps at one decisive point. "Entice him" introduces both the bribe and the threat. This verb, *patti,* frequently found in connection with seduction of a virgin, also occurs with reference to Yahweh's relationship with a wayward people and even with his prophets. Jeremiah complained bitterly that God had overpowered him and seduced him in the same way a virgin is raped (Jeremiah 20:7), and Ezekiel employed the verb to describe God's deception of his prophets (Ezekiel 14:9). Within wisdom literature the verb assumed special significance; it describes a foolish person who is easily misled. In Psalm 78:36 the word refers to flattery, the means of deceit, and stands in synonymous parallelism with *kazab,* to lie.

The Philistines offered Delilah a fabulous amount of silver. Each official promised her as much silver as Micah the Danite stole from his mother, eleven hundred pieces. The astronomical bribe left Delilah speechless, at least for the moment. The story withholds her response to the Philistines; her subsequent actions leave no doubt about the positive manner in which she received their offer. For so much money, she regained the use of her tongue rapidly.

Delilah's virgin attempt to discover Samson's source of strength borrowed heavily from the language of the Philistine officials, with one important difference. She omitted their allusion to overpowering Samson, and concentrated on the secret of his strength that prevented binding and afflicting him. Samson embarked on the path of teasing his beloved, confident that

Delilah's questions grew out of profound love and a desire to keep him for herself. Milton has Delilah defend her actions thusly:

> (I) sought by all means, therefore,
> How to endear, and hold thee to me firmest:
> No better way I saw than by importuning
> To learn thy secrets, get into my power
> Thy key of strength and safety (795–799).

Such an understanding of Samson's assumptions about Delilah's intentions suggests that he was not a total fool, but one blinded by love.

Samson teased Delilah three times before his fatal surrender of the clue to mastering him. These brief accounts are fraught with repetition; a few words suffice to describe the action. Both Samson and Delilah latched on to certain phrases and used them relentlessly: "then I shall be weak and become like any other man," "the Philistines are upon you, Samson," "Philistines were hiding in the inner chamber," "you have mocked me and spoken lies," and so forth. The description of the final disclosure surpasses all the others in its fourfold use of a single phrase. Delilah accused Samson of pretending love but guarding his *heart.* Later Samson told her *all his heart,* and when she saw that he had told her *all his heart,* she sent for the Philistines and informed them that he had told her *all his heart.* Samson teased her three times. Delilah used this awful phrase three times.

The false solutions to Samson's strength progress in the third disclosure dangerously close to the source of his strength. Samson focused attention upon his hair; from this point on, he faced no alternative but to divulge the full truth. So long as he dallied with peripheral matters, like being bound with seven fresh bowstrings or new ropes, Samson maintained a safe distance between love's frivolity and complete capitulation. Even within the first two tests Samson varied his language significantly. "If they bind me" becomes in the second test "if they *really* bind me." In addition, the personal pronouns change within the four answers in an important manner: twice "If *they* bind me" occurs, then "If *you* weave," and finally "If *I* be shaven." Use of the infinitive absolute strengthens Samson's language and implies that he has ceased mockery of Delilah.

The third test of Samson's strength foreshadows the final test in another way. Samson slept (on Delilah's knees) while she sought to weaken him by weaving the seven locks of his hair into the loom and cloth, and Delilah made him sleep on her knee when she divested him of his precious locks. Milton describes the scene beautifully.

> Softened with pleasure and voluptuous life,
> At length to lay my head and hallowed pledge
> Of all my strength in the lascivious lap
> Of a deceitful concubine, who shore me
> Like a tame wether, all my precious fleece,
> Then turned me out ridiculous, despoiled
> Shaven, and disarmed among my enemies (534–540).

In making use of the Philistine lords' language, Delilah omitted a significant word, the reference to mastering Samson. When she berated Samson for mocking her lovelessly, Delilah left out the major portion of their speech that had become her own through frequent use. Now she simply asked that he tell her wherein his strength was great. All reference to binding and afflicting was erased from her lips, which actively pushed Samson to hatred of his existence.

The secret that Samson had guarded zealously until Delilah's successful onslaught of his patience comes as something of a surprise to the most attentive listener or reader. It returns to an element of the saga that has been ignored since the opening episode. Samson attributed his great strength to a Nazirite vow. Apart from the birth narrative, nothing in the saga reinforces this interpretation of his special power. Instead, the spirit of Yahweh enabled him to perform all his mighty works. In every instance this spirit takes control of one who would be no match for his opponent without this power from God. Furthermore, nothing in Samson's conduct suggests that he took a Nazirite vow seriously. Instead, he played an active part in wedding festivities where wine would have flowed freely, and he ate honey which he had gathered from a lion's carcass. In addition, he scarcely could have avoided dead bodies, since, like the Canaanite warrior goddess Anat, he waded in the gore of slain soldiers.[25]

The narrator recognized the conflict between the alternative explanations of Samson's strength, and sought to identify the two viewpoints. He explained the immediate effect of Samson's haircut as a departure of his strength, but proceeded to inform us that Samson did not know the Lord had departed from him. In truth, the two interpretations are not wholly irreconcilable. One could argue that the uncut hair merely symbolized divine favor; once that hair was cut, Samson lost God's special presence.

The second scene of this fourth episode, though brief in scope, describes the end toward which Samson had been marching inevitably since his first glance at a beautiful woman. The Philistines' long vigil from the security of an inner chamber finally paid off, and they rushed upon a weakened Samson and rescued him from the afflictions imposed on him by a woman he loved. These triumphant lords gouged out Samson's eyes and took him to gateless Gaza. The rabbis caught a glimpse of the rare irony in this fact. They remarked that "In Gaza he first went whoring; in Gaza he was a prisoner."[26] Keenly sensitive to Samson's blind state, Milton has him exclaim:

> O loss of sight, of thee I must complain!
> Blind among enemies! O worse than chains,
> Dungeon or beggary, or decrepit age!
> Light, the prime work of God, to me is extinct. . . .
> Prison within prison, inseparably dark? (66–70, 153–154)

Fastened with bronze chains, Samson became a grinder at the prison in Gaza. His fall from divine favor resulted in a changed vocation. A Nazirite became a grinder, presumably performing chores normally entrusted to dumb animals.[27]

The story does not stop there. Indeed, even the succinct description of Samson's humiliation looks ahead to his recovery. This marvelous sentence hastens the saga to its denouement.

"But the hair of his head began to grow after it had been cut

(16:22)."[28] With one sweep of his brush, the artist has extinguished ominous clouds with the sun's radiance. Samson, the solar one, will rise again. Darkness, blindness, cannot stay the mighty Samson's hand.

The final scene reports Samson's return to divine favor. The setting constitutes a remarkable spiritual event, a sacrifice honoring the Philistine god Dagon who had given them victory over the Danite hero. Apart from the name of the deity, this celebration could have taken place in any Israelite camp. In the thinking of Israelite and Philistine, the deity determined the outcome of battle.[29] When he granted success, proper gratitude had to be expressed. This description of the Philistine sacrifice to Dagon breathes a remarkable spirit of tolerance. It suffers in no way from direct polemic against Dagon or his appreciative devotees.

At a sacrifice lauding Dagon for conquering Samson, it was proper that the subjected Danite demonstrate his bondage. The festive atmosphere prompted certain persons to suggest that they call Samson to make sport before them. Apparently these Philistines who were so eager to make fun of Samson had imbibed sufficient wine to loosen their tongues and entangle their speech. In any case, they used two distinct verbs for "making sport" as if the wine had gone to their brains.[30] Samson was called, and made sport. But the sport that he made moved closer and closer to grim agony for one and all.

Having entertained the enemy with mock feats of strength, Samson sought a place of rest between the two main columns that supported the structure upon which the Philistines sat. Their clamor failed to drown out Samson's faint plea for divine remembrance and renewed strength. His God heard that desperate prayer and rushed to Samson's aid. Armed with faith alone, Samson grasped the columns and fell beneath the rubble.

Half a verse suffices to describe the irony inherent within Samson's death. Blind, shackled, ridiculed, Samson slew more Philistines in his death than during his lifetime. Such a departure brought Samson's life to a fitting close.

The final comment in the story throbs with pathos, but one

must search for it beneath the surface of the narrative report. The latter notes that Samson's brothers and kinsmen retrieved his body and buried it in Manoah's grave. We wish to emphasize what fails to appear in these few words. First, Samson's father did not make this painful journey to Gaza. Indeed, the story implies that he had already died. Second, Samson died without progeny. His brothers, not his sons, went for Samson's body. Other narrators might have speculated about the old father's disappointment over his wayward son whose coming presaged marvelous events. Instead, he or she lets Manoah follow his nameless wife into obscurity.

A final word about Samson's brothers seems called for, since their mention in this context was wholly unexpected. Presumably, Manoah's wife gave birth to sons other than Samson. Once her reproach was taken away, she gave her husband sons and daughters with regularity. Alternatively, we may understand the word for brothers as a free rendering of uncles or kinsmen. Regardless of our interpretation of this word, their deed has no ambiguity. They return Samson to his father's side. In life, Philistine women came between them; in death only maggots and worms will do so.

To sum up, the Samson saga consists of four episodes. Each illustrates a different relationship between Samson and a woman. On the one hand, Samson's mother represents the ideal Israelite wife and mother. Over against a filial devotion to her, Samson enters upon competing relationships with foreign women. His first encounter depicts the power of physical attraction. The second represents sexual gratification on a casual basis. The third illustrates unreciprocated love. The saga wrestles with competing loyalties: parents versus lovers, charisma versus passion, Israelite versus Philistine. Samson's reasons for preferring lovers whose allegiance belonged to gods other than the Lord remain as enigmatic as his riddle, to which we now turn.

Chapter Three
The Riddles

If any truth resides in the popular sentiment that "the lion of the village must be first in success with the female sex, first in bodily strength, courage, and fondness for brawling, and first in mother wit,"[1] Samson qualifies as lion of Zorah. Having achieved remarkable success in gaining the hand of the lovely Timnite, he had little need to demonstrate his mighty physical strength, which none questioned. Still in doubt, however, was Samson's mental capacity. The riddle contest offered him a splendid opportunity to prove his superior wit.

Precisely what was at stake in the seemingly innocent challenge thrown out by a confident bridegroom? To answer this question, we must take a close look at the nature and function of riddles in the ancient world. Once we have gained some insight into the essential character of riddling, we shall be in a position to comprehend the riddle contest preserved in the Samson saga.

The Nature and Function of Riddles

Riddles depend upon language's ambiguity.[2] They communicate on two levels at the same time. Let us take the famous Sphinx riddle as an example: "What goes on four legs in the morning, two legs at noon, and three legs in the evening?" The language, though baffling because of its enigmatic character, makes perfect sense on the surface level. "Legs" "morning, noon, and evening" can be understood literally without straining anyone's credulity excessively. We shall call this the common or "appearance" level of comprehension. Another level of understanding penetrates beneath the surface to the essence of the language. We shall refer to this level as "essence" or special language. In this understanding of the statement, the word "legs" is a cipher, that is, sign language. Accordingly, one searches for something that functions as a leg.

Similarly, the temporal expressions constitute ciphers for life's stages (infancy, maturity, old age). Once Oedipus grasped the import of these ciphers, he was able to interpret the Sphinx's riddle. A child crawls on all fours, an adult walks erect, and an elderly person gains support from a walking cane.

Inasmuch as the language in riddles communicates on two levels simultaneously, we can say that it intentionally deceives. Essential to riddles is the setting of a trap. They endeavor to mislead by offering special language that masquerades as common language. Riddles therefore function to reinforce esoteric lore: Special groups or clans retain their uniqueness by use of ciphers known only to them.

It follows that riddles establish worth or identity rather than native intelligence. In an era when clan identity insured the wellbeing of an entire group, riddles provided an excellent means of assuring a group's integrity. Of course, other devices also enabled one group to identify outsiders. For example, the famous "shibboleth" test in Judges 12:6 rests on the different pronunciation of a key sibilant (s/sh). Presumably, linguistic skills varied with the region, so that a particular way of pronouncing a certain word betrayed one's real loyalty.

Since riddles penetrate the appearance to actual function or essence, a vital connection with myth arose early. The latter also endeavors to describe reality in a vocabulary that is foreign to the world it signifies. Mythic language describes eternity in temporal expressions, characterizes heaven in earthly language. Myth communicates transcendence by careful reference to finite existence. Accordingly, one must interpret myths, that is, elucidate the deeper meaning concealed within mythic lore. Here again, an impulse toward esoteric knowledge surfaces, for myths depend upon informed interpreters for their power and sway over human lives. Offensive conduct and trivial language must be explained away and impregnated with significant content. Otherwise myths soon lose their hold over people's minds.

Sometimes riddles transform myths into their own category of enigma. A well-known example suffices. In an ancient myth a certain priest was commanded to offer up what was noblest and what was basest. Perceptively, he sacrificed a tongue. For the sublimest gift, a kind word, comes from the tongue, as also does the basest language, a curse or betrayal. This mythic narrative has been transformed into a riddle: What instrument produces that which is the noblest and the basest on earth?

It is even possible for riddles to dispense with words altogether. In place of linguistic ciphers, sign language communicates to the alert interpreter. A single example will illustrate this point. A certain story, preserved in entirely different cultural and geographical areas, tells of a young ruler who sought counsel from his aged father about ways of improving his rule over the kingdom. Fearing that he might jeopardize himself or his son, the old man walked into his garden and systematically uprooted all older plants, leaving the very young in place to reach maturity unhindered. The messenger reported to the king that his father had not said a word. Description of his actions, however, communicated the point forcefully—remove the elderly statesmen and replace them with youthful leaders.

As the above story illustrates, at times one must be careful not to communicate with enemies, potential or real. Riddles supplied a way to circumvent the danger inherent in political advice, where one must see that the right ears hear what is intended for them. A certain risk accompanied every riddle. In truth, a convincing case has been made for connecting riddles and demonic powers. A net was essential to riddles in their inception; malevolent forces had a grim sense of humor. They offered anyone life for successfully unraveling a riddle, but failing this, the contestant received the death sentence. One can only guess how many valiant men in Greek legend lost their lives before Oedipus broke the power of the dreaded Sphinx.

One area in which demonic forces held sway was magic. Riddles seem to be as old as a magical worldview, and perhaps originated with it. Malevolent deities sought to enhance their power through magic; men and women, on the other hand, endeavored to manipulate those powerful forces by means of magic. One sure way of controlling deities for one's own best interests was to gain access to their names. The struggle to guard that sacred name from profanation or magical use seems to have fascinated people of many different cultures. The motif constitutes a universal quest, both ancient and comparatively modern. For example, it has given birth to the story of Rumpelstiltskin. Here, as in many stories within Egyptian, Mesopotamian, and Israelite literature the gods stand guard over their names lest they be used as sources of power. These gods seem bent on playing a game of "cat and mouse" with humans, to whom they offer clues to the discovery of their names. In this grim game, riddles function as a significant means of posing clues without exceptional risk to the deity so inclined.

An important reason for using ciphers is to avoid straight talk. In the area of eroticism, riddles flourish. They enable one to carry on polite conversation that conceals the bawdiest of senses from uninformed persons. Double entendre, the use of double meanings, is used profusely in riddling, particularly since sex and religion constitute the two favorite topics of riddles.

It follows that weddings supply a perfect occasion for the posing of riddles, both by the groom and by the bride. In fact, European tales abound in which a hero must demonstrate his right to the king's daughter by solving any riddle she may pose, or alternatively, by giving her a riddle that she cannot interpret. For such a prize, the risk of life and limb seemed a mere trifle.

Besides priestly circles, the royal court, and wedding contests, another setting for riddles was the school. In time this shift in locus was accompanied by a more significant transformation of riddles into idle jest. Here the riddle became a simple means of amusement, a device to while away the hours. Another important shift took place simultaneously: Riddles assumed a pedagogic role. Implicit in this new function of riddles was wide dissemination of esoteric lore, so that what was special language lost its cipher quality. Furthermore, other literary forms joined hands with riddles, chief of which was the "difficult or impossible question." Ultimately, catechisms incorporated elements of riddles, particularly because of the challenge inherent within the testing of one's wits.

We have claimed that riddles underwent a decisive change when pedagogs seized them for instructional use. What was the precise nature of this change? To answer this question, we need to clarify the fundamental presupposition of riddling.

To ancient peoples, the spoken word contained a numinous quality. It constituted the chief contact with the deity, the one who created all wielders of the word. In sacred utterance men and women proclaimed their likeness to God. Since language was fraught with immense power for good or ill, one's word became a sacred bond. The lie represented betrayal of trust. How, then, could one communicate with special persons without placing language's sanctity in jeopardy?

In response to this question, society developed a system of signs that functioned equivocally. From that moment language became a tool of simultaneous deception and communication. In time the peculiar danger inherent within any symbolic system, and particularly critical to the riddling process, constituted an Achilles' heel—special meanings once divulged became common knowledge. The freshness of discovered relationships gave way to time-worn metaphors, and an avaricious spirit pounced upon such newfound knowledge and put it to personal advantage. The result, highly similar to the advertising industry's tendency to borrow special vocabulary—of rebellious youth, the counterculture, and ethnic groups—for financial profit, drained riddling of its crucial components. The consequent bastardization of the mother tongue of special groups led to disgust and eventual abandoning of the terminology in favor of another set of symbols. Inevitably, the ciphers came to function univocally in the reverse sense of the original intention. Few linguistic systems can bear such heavy cargo for long. Impoverishment naturally follows.

In the ensuing hostility and linguistic lethargy or despair a decision often occurs that spells doom for the previous understanding of the word as sacred: Outright deceit replaces semantic equivocation. Henceforth, the lie dominates, and the word is stripped both of its dread and of its potential for excitement. Language now becomes unidimensional, and open deceit replaces linguistic ambiguity. This shift in anthropology bears special fruit; it produces a society that forgets the essential meaning of reality, one held in bondage to calculated lies. Integrity in the service of the author of truth ceases to control life and thought; instead, obeissance is offered at the feet of mendacity, for it pays.

In time a decisive change takes place in the process of education. Prior to this revolution in human understanding the aim of education was to discover worth and to discern ways in which essential relationships between different things could be expressed. Education sought the essence rather than appearance; it attempted to penetrate beneath outward manifestation to inner substance, and to encapsulate that wondrous discovery in a vehicle that both preserved mystery and divulged truth. As a direct result of the shift in learning's goal, knowledge came to be viewed in terms of facts that one apportions as a druggist dispenses pills. All knowledge then becomes utilitarian; it functions to indoctrinate. In the end, sectarian authority and interests gain complete control over education, which becomes indoctrination. Such victory over the Sphinx was indeed a Pyrrhic one.

Possibly the saddest result of this change concerns the general mood that characterizes learning. Rote memory of catechisms hardly compares with the excitement of fresh discovery typical of riddling. The person who poses a riddle behaves like a child who holds a butterfly in cupped hands. Pure excitement fills the soul. "I have found something," the discoverer cries triumphantly, "and wish to share it with those worthy of such profundity."

The revolution that we have discussed took place over and over, rather than once for all time. Wherever a group lost its fondness for shared mystery in favor of controlled knowledge, or considered the risks of discovery too great, that shift in worldview took place. New generations and other localities restored the old way of viewing things, so that we cannot give a convenient date for the great revolution. But that does not negate our claim that riddling constantly fought against insurmountable odds.

We have not mentioned the conflict between the popular and learned impulses within the riddling tradition. Ironically, riddles gave voice to the folk spirit and represented the poetic insights of rare scholars. This magnetic force sufficiently powerful to attract the simplest peasant and profoundest scholar explains why few can resist the challenge to solve a riddle. The joy of discovery turns learning into pure pleasure. To repeat an earlier observation: The solving of a riddle demonstrates worth.

In a sense riddles constitute an examination. Between examiner and examined stands a decisive test, a riddle, which can and must be unraveled. Successful students demonstrate their worth and earn credentials that open up a fuller life. Those who fail to meet the challenge posed by the test experience disgrace; in times past, they would also have felt the painful rod of an angry teacher.

The courtroom analogy complements the one borrowed from the classroom. In the law court successful probing of the unknown snatches a life from the threat of death or establishes guilt beyond a reasonable doubt. Whereas in an academic setting the examiner knows the answers and the one undergoing a test may or may not, in the criminal court the examiner feels around in partial darkness and must discover what the person under examination knows to be the truth. Both analogies illustrate different relationships between the examiner and examined that occur within the act of riddling.[3]

This description of the phenomenon called riddling derives from sources other than the Old Testament. If our assumption is correct that riddles are universal, we may validly illuminate biblical *chidot* from the wider world of enigmas. However, we now turn to consider *biblical* contexts in which riddles and related forms appear.

Riddles in the Old Testament

We confront an enigma at the outset. On the one hand, an ancient text (Numbers 12:8) intimates that normal revelatory discourse took place by means of riddles *(b^echidot)*. On the other hand, an astonishing paucity of riddles has survived in the Hebrew canon.[4] Even if we allow for the possibility that Israel's canonical self-understanding would hardly have favored double entendre, particularly where the erotic sense had become familiar to everyone, the sparsity of riddles demands explanation.

We shall begin our investigation with Numbers 12:8, the claim that God usually communicated with prophets in dark sayings, enigmas, riddles. The larger context of this use of "riddles" consists of a challenge to Moses' leadership, and hence, his uniqueness before God and the people. This questioning of Moses' status arose from the unlikeliest source of all, his brother and sister. Aaron's and Miriam's complaint went deeper than their ostensible cause for concern, namely Moses' marriage to a Cushite woman. Their real anxiety fell into the domain of charisma, that is, of worth. They articulated that concern in a question: "Has the Lord indeed spoken only through Moses? Has he not spoken through us also?" (12:2, RSV) The Lord quickly recognized that this challenge ultimately fell at his feet, since Moses merely functioned under divine appointment. Thus he issued a stern demand that Aaron and Miriam prepare for an ordeal: "Come out, you three, to the tent of meeting" (12:4, RSV).

The divine resolution of the "contest" underscored Moses' unique worth. God accomplished the elevation of Moses by making a sharp distinction between revelatory media afforded him and "the other prophets." With them God customarily speaks in visions or dreams. Moses, on the other hand, converses with God face to face, clearly and not in riddles. To him God has entrusted his house, and more than a glimpse of the divine form.

The decisive difference concerns the passive manner in which prophets receive God's word, as opposed to Moses' active participation in the revelatory experience. During dreams and visions one is acted upon from without; consequently, the revealed word must be opened before clarification occurs. Moses, however, asks pertinent questions during the revelatory moment; as a result, he utters God's actual words.

The precise conflict within prophetic movements reflected in Numbers 12:8 need not concern us here. Our aim is to demonstrate the claim that at least one stream of tradition looked upon riddles as normal revelatory communication. Such language had to be opened.

In one text (Psalm 49:4), the root *pth* (to open) occurs with reference to *chidot,* riddles.[5]

> I will incline my ear to a proverb *(mashal);* I will solve *('eptah)* my riddle *(chidati)* to the music of the lyre. (RSV)

Similarly, Psalm 78:2 uses *pth* in close relationship with *chidot.* Here the psalmist opens his mouth with a proverb and utters dark sayings from old. The actual content resembles creedal recitations of past history, which approximates a negative historical retrospect.[6] A nation recalls its weaker moments, which seem to linger in the national conscience as a kind of spiritual chastisement. Synonymous parallelism in this verse justifies our appeal to this context, although the two terms (translated proverb and riddle) are not precise equivalents. The riddle *(chidah)* must be opened. In it God breaks the silence of eternity and couches his speech in mystery that conceals and invites interpretation.

Israel's sages saw their task as the mastering of the art of opening dark sayings. The programmatic introduction (Proverbs 1:1–7) to the first collection of proverbs in the book by that name (Proverbs 1:1—9:18) concludes:

to understand a proverb *(mashal)* and a figure *(melitsah)*, the
words of the wise and their riddles *(chidot)* (1:6, RSV).

Similarly, Jesus ben Sira characterized scribes in his day as
persons who, among other things, penetrate the subtleties of
parables, seek out hidden meanings of proverbs, and are at
home with obscurities of parables (Sirach 39:2–3). Daniel readily admitted the power inherent within a knowledge of such
mysteries (8:23). He predicted that a king of bold countenance,
one who understood riddles *(chidot),* would wreak havoc among
God's saints.[7]

Israel even had a monarch whose mastery of the art of
opening riddles became legendary. The explicit purpose of the
Queen of Sheba's visit was to test Solomon with impossible
questions, or riddles *(bᵉchidot).*[8] Of course Solomon answered
all her questions satisfactorily, for "there was nothing hidden
(neʾlam) from the king which he could not explain to her" (1
Kings 10:3; 2 Chronicles 9:2—RSV). In this case the finding out
of the riddles required no effort at all. Consequently, the story
dispensed with the verb "to find out" *(mtsʾ),* and used the ordinary word *ngd* (to tell).

In sum, these biblical contexts use *chidot* with reference to
(1) contest literature; (2) enigmatic sayings, allegories and proverbs; (3) creedal lore in some respects comparable to a catechism; (4) impossible or difficult questions; and (5) actual
riddles. Furthermore, they provide some technical vocabulary
of riddling in ancient Israel, specifically the terms open *(pth),*
find out *(mtsʾ),* and tell *(ngd* in the hiphil). These texts also
inform us that "riddles" were at home in the cult, the royal
court, and the school.

Several literary forms participate in certain qualities that
form the essence of riddles. While the proverb, which Cer-
vantes characterized as "a short sentence founded on long experience,"[9] functions differently from the riddle, the two have
come together in a few instances. Perhaps the wedding came
because each made use of the other's materials now and again.
In any case, numerical proverbs occasionally harbor earlier
riddles.

At first glance certain items that have been joined together
in ascending fashion strike one as wholly dissimilar.

> Three things are too wonderful for me;
>   four I do not understand:
> the way of an eagle in the sky,
>   the way of a serpent on a rock,
> the way of a ship on the high seas,
>   and the way of a man with a maiden (Proverbs 30:18–19,
> RSV).

What a strange conglomeration we find in this clever proverb
(cf. Wisdom of Solomon 5:9–12). We ask: What have eagle, serpent, ship, and man-woman to do with one another? Closer
analysis teaches us that each of the four movements leaves no
trace, no tell-tale marks of paths taken. Furthermore, the word
"way" *(derek)*[10] also connotes sovereignty, a term that frequently designated man's conquest of woman.

In such proverbs emphasis falls upon the final member (in
this instance the remarkable entry of a penis into a vulva
without subsequently leaving any trace of its presence). The
other items, although highly appropriate functionally, merely
point beyond themselves to the climactic one. This example
demonstrates numerical proverbs' power to penetrate beneath
external manifestation (appearance) to a deeper level of intrin-
sic relationship (essence). In a decisive sense each object (eagle,
serpent, ship, man-woman) functions similarly, and thus par-
ticipates in a common mystery. By signifying a single relationship of such diversified objects, the proverb offers the slightest
hint of a harmonious universe. One can easily turn such numerical proverbs into riddles. But this cannot be accomplished
without a complete *transformation* of the proverb. Although
ciphers occur within numerical proverbs ("way" in this one),
the intention to deceive hardly accompanies them.

Impossible tasks or difficult questions also share one important characteristic with riddles. Fascination with the impossible arose early in human history; the attempt to determine
boundaries of the possible represented a striving for security by
ascertaining the certain and the achievable. Virgil's clever dis-
missal of the absurd with "Then the stag will fly and the buck

fn?

will give milk" amounted to his recognition of propriety as a significant feature of daily life. Certain things simply cannot take place, no matter how much one may wish them.

The author of Job appreciated this fact; the much-maligned Job concedes that a stupid person will acquire understanding "when a wild ass's colt is born a man" (11:12). One's response to such questions, or in these instances, assertions, manifests surprise, nay astonishment. This evocation of disbelief corresponds to the proper reaction to riddles, for one looks upon them with scepticism. Riddles strain one's credulity. When impossible questions employ ciphers from riddle traditions, affinities between the two literary genres increase. In short, the inclusion of impossible questions with riddle collections seems proper from one perspective, at least.

Contest literature, sometimes called question-and-answer dialogue, often treads on the perimeters of riddles. To be sure, such texts hardly qualify as dialogue in the sense in which Plato used the term. But one observes in this genre a mechanical concatenation of questions and answers, each complete in itself, although chain-like units (sorites) do occur. Particularly useful in Homeric and scriptural exegesis, the question-and-answer dialogue rivals catechism in popularity among ancient educators.

An exquisite example of contest literature survives within 1 Esdras.[11] Here Darius' three guardsmen offer competing answers to a single question: "What is strongest?" Their eloquent defence of wine, king, woman, and truth as strongest possesses immense entertainment value. Rhetoric soars to marvelous peaks, especially in the form of rhetorical question and humor.

Both riddles and question-and-answer dialogues share a common atmosphere, strife, and a technique of overcoming opposition, deceptive understatement. It has even been claimed that riddles should be subsumed under the larger category of question-and-answer dialogue; they then would represent the more popular side of such contests while *aporia* would constitute the learned aspect.

In many respects the question-and-answer dialogue resembles a catechism. The decisive difference seems to be more formal than substantive; we refer to the literary guise of a debate between famous persons as opposed to the simple question-and-answer format of catechisms. Substantive differences exist, however: While catechisms depend upon scripture, creed, or theological dogma, question-and-answer dialogues range freely over the wide field of human knowledge.

At what point do catechism and riddle meet? Whenever the former goes beyond a mere desire to inform, it joins a riddle in penetrating beneath the surface of reality. Since transcendant truth can only be *grasped* in other-worldly images, but must be *presented* in this-worldly discourse, some means of achieving this miraculous translation must be discovered. The riddle provides a ready-made vessel for this hazardous trip between two worlds, even if at the expense of spontaneity. Because theological data can be learned, surprise, so essential to riddle, vanishes. Still a catechism can occasionally sustain remarkable religious power. We think, for instance, of the moving response between a father and various members of a family, contained within a Jewish passover haggadah, " 'aehad mi yode 'a" ("One, who knows it?").[12] This rehearsal of important facets of religious memory leads up to recitation of the thirteen divine attributes that were communicated to Moses on the occasion of God's self-manifestation (Exodus 34:6–7).

So far we have laid no stress upon the mood evoked by these literary forms. With some reservation, we would argue for the following correlations of moods and genres: riddle—malice; numerical proverbs—eros; question-and-answer dialogue—humor, often grim; impossible questions—wonder. Often more than one mood appears within a given literary type, but not at the expense of a dominant spirit.

Riddles Within the Samson Saga

Having examined the nature of riddle and similar literary types, we are now in a position to take a close look at the riddles contained in the Samson narrative. We have already taken note of the fondness of initial "m" in Samson's first riddle and the Philistine's reply. The following chart represents this special stylistic feature.

SAMSON'S RIDDLE	THE PHILISTINES' RIDDLE
"Food came from the eater; sweetness came from strength."	"What is sweeter than honey and what is stronger than a lion?"
meha'okel (from the eater)	mah (what)
ma'akal (food)	matoq (sweet)
(u)me'az (from the strong)	midbas (than honey)
matoq (sweetness)	(u)meh (what)
	me'ari (than a lion)

In Samson's riddle only one word lacks an initial "m", although that word occurs twice. The Philistines' answer has only one word without introductory "m", and it derives from Samson's riddle. Both riddles use only six words. Both also employ parallelism, but of a different kind. Whereas Samson's riddle uses synonymous parallelism, the response to it resorts to ascending parallelism.

Samson's Riddle

Our search for ciphers in Samson's riddle comes off successfully, for four words belong to the category of special language. "Eater" and "food," "strength" and "sweetness" point beyond themselves to a deeper dimension of reality. Of course, in context we know that the lion was the eater and honey came from it. Since the two halves of the riddle stand in exact parallelism, we also recognize that the lion was the strong one from which came the sweet tasting honey. We have already been told that Samson scraped honey from a lion's carcass and shared it with his parents, or if we give credence to Josephus' account, with the beautiful Timnite who had captivated Samson's eyes.[13]

The Philistines' answer seizes upon the contextual ciphers and identifies their referents. Surprisingly, their response ap-

pears in interrogative form. Perhaps we ought to recognize this
question form as a way of emphasizing the simplicity of Samson's riddle. By stating their answer in interrogative form, the
Philistines imply that any fool would have been able to solve
Samson's riddle. Later rabbinic practice of answering difficult
questions with questions derives from a similar impetus, a desire to impress the interrogator with the simplicity of the question.

This reversal of sentence form in Samson's riddle and its
answer has prompted several interpreters to deny the presence
of a riddle in the story. We readily admit that the normal form
for a riddle is interrogative and that its answer appears in a
declarative sentence. But we insist that exceptions often occur
in the form of the riddle and in the answer. Although Samson
expressed his riddle in declarative form, its enigmatic character virtually transforms it into a question. In truth, the riddle
functions interrogatively. That is, it provokes a response and
demands a reaction similar to an interrogative sentence. The
riddle breathes an unexpressed "What is it that?" Conversely,
the Philistines' answer in question form functions rhetorically
like a statement, while at the same time posing a further riddle.

Samson's riddle has been attacked on still another ground.
A riddle must provide a genuine clue that makes the question
inherently answerable. Furthermore, riddles must belong to
common experience. Samson's riddle hardly meets either criterion. The action of the thirty Philistines reinforces the impossi-
bility of Samson's riddle; presumably, too, such an occurrence
as honey in a lion's carcass was extremely rare, despite popular
belief to the contrary.

We have but one thing to say to such critics. The narrative
demands just such a riddle. We encounter a Neck Riddle in this
story. The gravity of the situation necessitates a riddle that
strains one's mental powers to the limit. In the Neck Riddle
one's life hangs in the balance. He or she must either answer
a riddle on penalty of death, or pose an insoluble riddle with the
same high stakes. Such riddles often derive from private expe-

rience. On the other hand, it should not be thought that Samson alone in human history obtained honey from a lion's carcass. Or, to state the same point differently, in saga, nothing prevents the same experience from taking place several times.

If Samson's riddle had been inherently answerable, the Philistines would not have resorted to threats to wheedle the answer from the Timnite. The story would necessarily have aborted. Since unanswerable riddles belong to a specific type of narrative resembling the Samson story, we can say with confidence that Samson actually posed a *riddle* to the Philistines. By identifying Samson's statement as a Neck Riddle, we blunt the force of the claim that "it was, in truth, a very bad riddle" or that it was really "a trivial conundrum invented to pose ingenuity."[14]

One example suffices to demonstrate the aptness of Samson's riddle: "The Princess Who Cannot Solve the Riddle."[15] In this story a hero on his way to a riddle contest for the hand of a lovely princess saw in turn a horse die from poisoning, a raven devouring bits of the carcass, and twelve men perish as a result of feasting on the raven. The hero coined a riddle that grew out of this extraordinary experience. It went: "One killed none and yet killed twelve." Although resorting to mastery of dreams the princess failed to discover the answer to the riddle, and she became the hero's wife.

Returning to Samson's riddle, we wish to insist that the context demands the answer provided by the Philistines. However, Samson's use of double entendre implies that other answers were possible. Indeed, his riddle contained deceptive clues that would have ensnared the Philistines if they had taken them at face value. To discover these alternative interpretations of the riddle, we must disregard the context completely. In all likelihood, the riddle antedates its context anyway.[16]

Samson's riddle relies upon an obscene double meaning.[17] On one level, the ciphers point to "vomit" as the answer to Samson's riddle: Food came from the eater; sweet things came from the strong person. Thus understood, the riddle refers to the aftermath of wedding festivities during which valiant young men were unable to retain such unaccustomed delicacies. Although the riddle constitutes a vivid *description* of baneful effects of overindulgence, it also presents a net to catch the unwary Philistine, and thus deserves the title "riddle." The thirty young men made their way cautiously around this trap set so cleverly by Samson.

On another level, the riddle suggests copulation. Such erotic thoughts naturally accompanied wedding festivities, and consequently posed the biggest snare for the Philistines. A veiled allusion to the sex act, the riddle uses the ciphers "eater" and "strong one" for the groom. Similarly, "food" and "sweetness" signify semen, which is sweet to the bride who "eats" the sperm. From man proceeds sperm which nourish woman; from a strong man goes semen that is pleasant to a wife.

An interesting text in Proverbs 30:20 throws light upon this erotic metaphor.

> This is the way of an adulteress:
> she eats, and wipes her mouth,
> and says, "I have done no wrong" (RSV).

In this marvelous characterization of a loose woman, two ciphers function euphemistically. Both "eat" and "mouth" point beyond themselves to an essential relationship, the functional similarity between eating and copulation.[18]

Proverbs 5:15–18 expands the metaphor to include drinking. In this instance, too, the author leaves no doubt about the erotic sense in which language of eating and drinking is used.

> Drink water from your own cistern,
>   flowing water from your own well.
> Should your springs be scattered abroad,
>   streams of water in the streets?
> Let them be for yourself alone,
>   and not for strangers with you.
> Let your fountain be blessed,
>   and rejoice in the wife of your youth,
> a lovely hind, a graceful doe (RSV).

Ciphers punctuate this little bit of useful advice: "drink," "water," "cistern," "springs," "fountain" and so forth.

This erotic language occurs in other literary complexes. For instance, Song of Solomon 4:12, 15 describe the beloved as a virginous fountain:

> A garden locked is my sister, my bride,
> a garden locked, a fountain sealed . . .
> a garden fountain, a well of living water,
> and flowing streams from Lebanon (RSV).

Even prophetic symbolism and ancient nomenclature bear witness to the popularity of such language. Deutero-Isaiah describes inhabitants of the southern kingdom as those who came from the waters of Judah (Isaiah 48:1), by which the prophet means Judah's sperm. In addition, the Greek text of Genesis 19:37 interprets the name Moab to mean "from the waters of my father" *(me'abi).* [19]

Extrabiblical parallels to such erotic ciphers reach as far back as the ancient Sumerian literature. Three proverbs suffice to demonstrate the presence of this language from earliest times.

> If his "food" be something (sexually) defiling,
> one should not be overwhelmed (?) by it . . .
> If his "food" be . . . "eggs," his ardour (?) will be . . .
> If his "food" be . . . "bones," his ardour (?) will be . . .

Despite the poor condition of these texts, enough has survived to recognize in them an attack against male prostitutes associated with cultic worship, and to understand "eggs" and "bones" as ciphers for male genitalia. [20]

In light of this abundance of evidence for an erotic use of language for eating and drinking, which can easily be supplemented from other cultures, we conclude that Samson's riddle contained a possible erotic answer. Once again, if the Philistines had fallen for this bait, Samson would have caught them in his well-hidden trap.

Samson's riddle may have set still another trap for the wary Philistines. [21] Canaanite texts attest a word *'ar* for honey, thus suggesting that Samson's clever saying may constitute a riddle of consonance, that is, a play on words. Thus interpreted, the word for food *(ma'akal)* derives from that for eater *('okel),* and the term for something sweet *('ari)* comes from the word also meaning lion *('ari)*. Samson's riddle would then call attention to the remarkable phonetic similarities in these words. According to this interpretation, the real riddle would consist of the relationship between the words for honey and lion, whereas the two other ciphers provide the clue to such an understanding of the riddle.

The Philistines' response demonstrates their capacity to steer clear of the various mines Samson had planted in their harbor. Refusing to follow a direct course to any one of the possible destinations, they chose a devious route that led them safely into port. The narrator provides no clue in regard to their ability to recognize these false solutions to Samson's riddle. Perhaps we should conclude that they understood the three obvious solutions, but saw in them misleading answers. Alternatively, the author may have intended to convey their stupidity by suggesting that the Philistines could not even discover the transparent answers to Samson's riddle. In any event, they refused to fall into a trap by answering before they had the solution confirmed from a reliable source.

The Philistines' Riddle

Since the Philistines clothe their answer in riddle form, we should probably not accuse them of general stupidity.

> What is sweeter than honey?
> What is stronger than a lion?

Although we cannot accept the old thesis that the lion symbolizes the animal circle in which the sun moves during the hottest season of the year, we can concede the presence of another riddle in this double question. Behind the Philistines' answer lies a familiar riddle that suggests the source of their information. "What is sweetest and strongest?" alludes to love's power and ecstasy. Heine has aptly described these two characteristics of love.

> The angels call it heavenly joy
> The demons call it hellish grief

> By men it love is called.
> O love, how bitter art thou,
> O love, how sweet thou art.

If one can legitimately render ʿaz with "cruel" or "bitter," the riddle gains considerable power. Then the implied riddle would read:

> What is sweeter (more desirable) than honey?
> What is more bitter (crueler) than a lion?

We concur in the objection that such a formulation is inferior to a hypothetical "What is sweeter than honey and bitterer than death?"[22] But we insist that riddles vary in their power to compel assent. Of course, a better riddle could have been formulated; but that does not rule out the possibility or likelihood that the Philistines' answer alludes to an old riddle.

The additional charge that such an interpretation of the riddle stands alone in biblical literature in its negative attitude toward sensual love hardly refutes the claim that a riddle lies beneath the surface of the Philistines' answer. Certainly Song of Solomon 8:6 expresses a similar sentiment:

> . . . for love is strong as death,
> jealousy is cruel as the grave.

Likewise Ecclesiastes 7:26–29 gives expression to powerful scepticism about the trustworthiness of women, who are in fact only one one-thousandth worse than men. From here it is only a tiny step to such expressions of love as cruel, for the experience is universal. Nor should we forget that the criticism of love stands alongside an exquisite praise of its sweetness, which too is universally experienced.

Samson's Retort

Samson's caustic response informs the Philistines that he has understood their implied riddle:

> Had you not plowed with my heifer,
> you would not have found out my riddle.

Their success in solving Samson's riddle has transformed love's sweetness into gall. The protasis, or conditional clause, con-

tains two ciphers (plowed and heifer). We can therefore turn
this half of his statement into a familiar riddle:

What fertile field is plowed, but not with oxen?

One would be hard put to discover a more apt description of the
sexual act. For this reason, the metaphor occurs in cultures as
diverse as the Canaanite fourteenth century population known
to us from the Amarna tablets, Mesopotamian, and Israelite.

In a letter from Rib-Addi of Byblos he writes that "My field
is like a woman without a husband, on account of its lack of
cultivation."[23] From the land of the Tigris and Euphrates riv-
ers we read:

> ". . . As for *me,* my vulva is a hillock,—*for me,*
> I, the maid, who will be its plower?
> My vulva is . . . wet ground *for me,*
> I, the queen, who will station there the ox?"
> "Lady, the king will plow it for you,
> Dumuzi, the king, will plow it for you."
> "Plow my vulva, my sweetheart."[24]

For the metaphor in Israelite literature, we need only look to
Song of Solomon 4:12.

> A garden locked is my sister, my bride,
> a garden locked, a fountain sealed.

Although this particular verse says nothing about plowing,
everyone knew that gardens had to be tilled.

Samson's garden had been cultivated by strangers. Now he
would let it lie fallow for the time being. Perhaps such a meaning lies behind his abusive metaphor for the beautiful Timnite.
The comparison between women and cows occurs elsewhere, in
the book of Amos (4:1), perhaps without negative connota-
tions.[25] Samson's use of the personal pronoun indicates the
precise point at which he feels offended. *His own* wife has
betrayed him. Others have plowed *his* garden. Furthermore, a
special irony fills the story. Samson's defeat comes because his
wife performed the task of an animal. Later, Samson will himself carry out the work of oxen.

A rabbinic story indicates clear dependence upon this biblical narrative. In a contest between certain Jews and Greeks the

latter obtained the correct answer by devious means, and were chided for plowing with the Jews' heifer.[26]

In all probability, then, we have three riddles in the Samson narrative. The first one belongs to the classification "Neck Riddle" and has several possible answers, only one of which satisfies the criterion of context. The other two riddles lie behind normal verbal interchange between Samson and his opponents. Since the actual riddles cannot be discovered apart from a transformation process, we cannot be absolutely certain the narrator understood the Philistines' answer and Samson's retort as riddles. Regardless, they satisfy formal requirements: They use ciphers that simultaneously communicate and ensnare.

In all three instances the riddles tread upon erotic subsurfaces, and therefore belong to wedding festivities. Their appropriateness to the setting does not rule out the possibility, nay likelihood, that they antedate their context, with the single exception of Samson's allusion to honey that he took from a lion's carcass. The Danite hero's ability to coin riddles and to recognize one in the Philistine's answer proves beyond doubt that Samson can lay claims upon the title, "Lion of the Village."

Chapter Four
The Tragic Dimension

Samson's fondness for Philistine women was matched by a powerful dislike of Philistines in general on Yahweh's part. This divine hostility toward non-Israelites characterizes both the framework of the narrative and the individual stories. Indeed, the Lord appears as one desiring to pick a fight with Philistines (14:4), into whose hands he has given his wayward people (13:1).

Manoah's loathing for a non-Israelite woman as a daughter-in-law equalled his son's desire for one. A loyal Yahwist and grateful father, Manoah could not fathom Samson's preference for a daughter of the uncircumcised Philistines. Presumably, Samson's mother shared her husband's sentiments, for she joined him as subject in the sentence that bristles with shock over their son's intentions to marry a Timnite (14:3).

The people of Judah concealed whatever hatred they felt for their rulers. Prudence told them that accomodation works wonders toward assuring security amidst servitude. In their judgment, subjection to Philistines constituted a fact of life which they did not wish to jeopardize. Underneath their servile behavior intense hatred may have seethed, but it never boiled over in the Samson narrative, not even when the men of Judah might have been able to capitalize upon Samson's victory at Ramath-lehi so as to throw off the Philistine yoke forever.

At first glance, Samson's frequent skirmishes with Philistines seem to link him with Manoah and his God as antagonists of the uncircumcised. Two qualifications must be made. First, the spirit of Yahweh seized Samson when he waged battle (with two exceptions: the great slaughter after the Philistines burned the Timnite woman and her father, and Samson's final act against himself and his enemies). Second, Samson's battles always occurred after an affront to his person. In short, he sought revenge from those who became his enemies.

Ius Talionis

Unlike Yahweh, who actively provoked Philistines to battle, Samson wished to live peacefully with them. The entire saga breathes a remarkable spirit of fair play *(ius talionis)*.[1] Samson seems not to have adhered to the principle that might determines right. Instead, he merely sought revenge for wrongs committed against him.

The sneak attack against thirty Askelonites came as a direct result of the treacherous manner in which the thirty Philistines obtained the answer to Samson's riddle. After the Timnite woman's father turned Samson away with the offer of a lovelier bride, Samson countered:

> This time I am innocent with regard to the Philistines when I do them harm (15:3).

Once his wholly justified retaliation culminated in the flaming death of his wife and her father, Samson again vowed only to get revenge, and afterwards to quit.

> If you act like this,
> I swear that I shall be avenged upon you,
> and afterwards I shall quit (15:7).

The last episode remains true to character. Samson's final prayer articulates this principle of fair play with a touch of grim irony.

> O Lord God, remember me, I pray,
> and strengthen me,
> just this time, O God, that I may avenge myself a vengeance from the Philistines for one of my two eyes (16:28).[2]

The Philistines, too, adhered to the principle of fair play on two occasions. After Samson destroyed their grain and olive harvest, they inquired about the guilty culprit and took revenge against the person who had prompted Samson's malicious act. Thus their cruel arson arose out of a desire for revenge rather than pure malice. Similarly, their conversation with the people of Judah magnified the retaliatory principle.

> We have come up to bind Samson,
> to do to him as he did to us (15:10).

Exceptions occurred, of course, but they grew out of cumulative provocations. In time Samson became their archenemy, and the Philistines of Gaza planned to seize him and put an end to his destructive ways. Likewise, the Philistine lords who paid Delilah to obtain the secret of his strength acted to rid themselves of an inveterate foe. Consequently the people praised their god for granting them victory over the one who had ravaged their land.

This willingness to give Philistines the benefit of the doubt, a sentiment in tension with the general attitude of the saga, finds its closest parallel in the Succession Narrative (2 Samuel 9—20; 1 Kings 1—2). Fleeing from Jerusalem and his rebellious son, David was accompanied by six hundred Gittites, that is citizens of Gath. When King David urged Ittai to remain in Jerusalem with Absalom, the newly proclaimed king, Ittai answered: "As the Lord lives, and as my lord the king lives, wherever my lord the king shall be, whether for death or for life, there also will your servant be" (2 Samuel 15:21, RSV). Such priceless loyalty from the people against whom Yahweh wished to provoke a skirmish stands as a sharp contrast to betrayal by David's own son.

Elsewhere biblical traditions depict Philistines as villains who dominated Israel and charged exorbitant prices for essential services. The old narratives about the ark poke fun at the Philistines who could not withstand Yahweh's fury and who got rid of the sacred ark in a desperate move to save their necks (1 Samuel 5—6). Similarly, the Philistines' Samson, the famed Goliath, became an object of derision. These stories hardly endeavor to present Philistines as men and women governed by a sense of fair play. Instead, these narratives are closer to those depicting Manoah as adamantly opposed to marriage with Philistines, and Yahweh as eager to instigate a fight with the uncircumcised inhabitants of Canaan.

Tragic Destiny

This tension within the Samson saga between open hostility toward Israel's oppressors and the care with which their cruelty is justified grows out of an awareness of the ambiguity of all human events. Both Samson and his antagonists seem moved by a force over which they have no control. One hesitates to call that power "Fate," but it functions to propel both the Timnite woman and Samson along the pathway that leads to destruction.

How else can we describe the plight in which the Timnite woman found herself? Caught up in the clutches of a power beyond her ability either to comprehend or to elude, this pitiful figure walked slowly but surely into a flaming death. Faced with a choice between kinship and the novelty of wedded bliss, and hastened to a decision by a terrifying threat, she took the inevitable step toward deceiving the only one who could have extricated her from the power of destiny.

The awful threat, "Entice your husband and tell us the riddle, lest we burn you and your father's house with fire" (14:15), really left her no option. The sequel to the episode makes it plain that she made the wrong choice. In this instance the wife preferred kinship to a foreigner, even if he were her husband. But that decision culminated in death for her and her father. Having escaped one terrible threat, she saw it implemented by other hands than those owned by the thirty companions to whom she had divulged Samson's secret.

Samson's choice was the opposite of that made by the Timnite woman. Confronted by a decision between parental wishes and the pulsing of his heart, or at the very least, the surging of sexual desire, he opted for the latter like any redblooded Danite. But this, too, was the wrong decision, as events demonstrated. It set into motion a series of conflicts that led step by step into Delilah's chamber, and ultimately to Manoah's grave.

The Samson saga, then, contains a sophisticated reading of

the complexity of human events, indeed, a sense of the inevitable. One can even speak of a slaughter of the innocents, despite what we have said about the saga's concern to magnify the justness of the causes resulting in calamity.

With touching simplicity the narrator introduced the lad who guided Samson to the pillars upon which the temple of Dagon rested. This lad, too, was someone's cause for rejoicing, hope for eternity. But his destiny, alas, was intricately woven into the fabric of Samson's life span, and he fell along with the mocking crowds. Through no fault of his own, the unfortunate youth went to his final resting place alongside the columns to which he had led Samson in search of rest, or so he thought.[3]

The men of Askelon, too, walked under a dark cloud of fate.[4] They could easily have been somewhere else when an angry Samson came in search of thirty festal garments and thirty linen garments. Like Sisera, these thirty fallen enemies had mothers or wives awaiting their safe return, and perhaps children also waited anxiously for their fathers. But a frustrated Samson interrupted the normal course of daily events for those households. In the case of Sisera, the poem provides a glimpse into his mother's heart. These thirty Askelonites merely function as extras, and no one asks what their death meant to other lives dear to them.

By far the most pitiful creature was the little sister of the lovely Timnite woman. Unnamed and undesired in spite of her ravishing beauty, this younger sister was bartered away by a self-serving father in the same way Lot offered his daughters to a lecherous mob rather than gain a reputation as one who ignored the ancient hospitality code. At another time and under other circumstances, this beautiful maiden might have exulted in Samson's wondrous feats, luxuriated in the pleasures of love, and given suck to his children. Instead, she lived with the hollow echo of her father's offer: "Is not her younger sister better than she? Let her be for you instead" (15:2). And before she had time to make peace with herself over Samson's rejection of the offer, she too succumbed to the roaring flames that engulfed her father's house.

The plight of this younger sister, and that of all of these

innocent victims of the developing hatred between Samson and his foes, approaches that of Jephthah's daughter. Indeed, this story about Jephthah's vow immediately precedes the Samson narrative and furnishes a sharp contrast, for in this instance a vow is kept at all costs (Judges 11:1—12:7).

The son of a harlot, Jephthah was driven away from his family and gathered a band of ruffians around himself. When Ammonites threatened the Gileadites, the terrified people of Gilead offered Jephthah leadership over them if he would deliver them from the enemy. Jephthah agreed, and began to negotiate with the Ammonites through messengers. Rehearsing Israel's history in Transjordan, Jephthah argued that since God had given the land of Gilead into Israel's hands they had merely received his gift. He pointed out that the Ammonites would have done the same thing if Chemosh had given the land to them. Therefore Jephthah called upon God, the Judge, to decide whose cause had merit.

The spirit of the Lord seized Jephthah, and he went to war against the Ammonites. To assure victory, he vowed that he would sacrifice whoever came forth from his house to greet him on his successful return home. The Lord gave Jephthah a glorious victory, and he went home in high spirits. But his jubilance faded quickly, for his only daughter ran to greet him. Jephthah told her about his vow, and made known his troubled spirit. His daughter asked only to be allowed to climb the mountains to bewail her virginity for two months. At the appointed time, she returned and her father fulfilled his vow to the Lord. Therefore, a custom of annual lamentation over the daughter's wasted virginity arose in Israel.

These figures approach a tragic dimension, if one understands the term broadly to refer to destiny over which one has no control. In a sense, Samson symbolizes a negative hero. He exemplifies one who betrays everything for which he had been given to a barren woman. His negative examples concern relationships with women and treatment of a solemn vow. The fascination with foreign women drives him closer and closer to defeat; Samson's willingness to risk his neck seems to derive from inner compulsion. In this behavior he differs little from classic tragic heroes who cannot turn their backs upon danger although they know it will destroy them.

In many respects Samson's inner compulsion to bring about his own collapse resembles the career of Israel's first king who also fell into the hands of the Philistines. Saul's fall from divine favor and desperate attempts to reclaim it approach the spirit of Greek tragedy. Even his oath brings a curse upon his own household (1 Samuel 14:29–30), and Jonathan has to be rescued at the people's expense. At last driven by madness, Saul's life story unfolds "a tragedy which in its final act rises to solemn grandeur."[5]

David's personal tragedy unfolds in a similar manner, beginning with his erotic venture with Bathsheba and the ensuing murder to cover up his crime. Events within his family happen as if driven by some powerful force bent on ripping apart the king's family.[6] In the end David's children suffer disgrace and murder, and the old king watches his own sons rebel against their father and repeat his libidinous behavior. This tragic story reaches its climax in a powerful lament over Absalom.

> O my son Absalom, my son, my son Absalom!
> Would I had died instead of you,
> O Absalom, my son, my son! (2 Samuel 18:33; H 19:1)

Comical Aspects

Certain features of the Samson saga resemble comedy more than tragedy, and thus warn against taking the latter too seriously. In some instances, comedy approaches the ludicrous, while in others it is closer to the whimsical. Whether mildly amusing or hilarious, the comic elements enliven the story in rich fashion.

The birth narrative constitutes a marvelous build-up that soon gives way to one unexpected disappointment after another. Having learned that Samson is destined to be a Nazirite, we expect him to excel in his religious vocation. What a surprise, therefore, when the son of promise behaves in total disregard of his religious calling. Did his parents forget to inform him of his marvelous destiny? Possessing an eye for foreign women, Samson brushed his parents aside as readily as he ignored his calling. From that moment forward he moved from one amusing scene to another.

As a result of his wager and the events it generated, Samson's wife was given to the best man, who was entrusted with the responsibility of looking out for Samson's interests. The next scene depicts Samson chasing after three hundred foxes with the aid of which he burnt the enemies' grain fields. Surely he could have found an easier method of setting fire to their life-sustaining crops. After that, Samson ran away and hid in a rocky crag; the picture of the mighty Danite warrior cowering in some remote recess is inherently funny. So is the thought of three thousand Judahites marching down to bind a single man who had hidden from the Philistines. Samson's choice of a fighting implement is ludicrous—an ass's jawbone scarcely serves as an appropriate weapon for the champion of just causes. Nor was Samson's makeshift drinking vessel exactly appropriate for one who had just secured a mighty deliverance; how he could have used some of the silver Delilah later pocketed from which to fashion a cup.

The entire Gaza episode furnishes light comic relief. The stage was set for disaster, but a satisfied lover demonstrated his virility in more ways than one. Amusing, too, is the Delilah episode in which Philistines hid in an inner chamber while Samson engaged in love play with his mistress. One by one the teasing incidents led up to the comical scene in which Samson slept on Delilah's knees while his seven locks were shaven. Of course Samson was a heavy sleeper! His punishment was equally funny. Having plowed with Philistine heifers from Gaza to the valley of Sorek, he now became a professional grinder. He thus does the work usually performed by women, oxen, or asses. Since he is now blind, Samson cannot even see Delilah spending the vast sum of silver. Of course she must have bought herself a wig with some of the money!

The final episode continues this humorous element. The

exuberant Philistines became slightly tipsy, and three thousand climbed on the roof of a single building. Samson made sport before them, but what unusual sport! Then the tables were turned, and the blind Danite did them in. The story closes with the most ludicrous scene of all. Danite kinsmen sifted through rubble in search of the body of their hero who had whimsically spoken of revenge for one of his two eyes and who had half-laughingly uttered his final words: "I shall die with the Philistines!" He must have found something slightly amusing in that grim fate, since he was accustomed to making his bed with their daughters. The story ends with a funeral march, and we are supposed to assume that the brothers found the real Nazirite in the Gazite ruins. We can only hope for their sake the search achieved success before the body began the process of decomposition.

We conclude, therefore, that a strong case can be made for viewing the Samson saga as a tragi-comedy. The two moods alternate throughout the story; neither tragedy nor comedy becomes sufficiently pronounced to drown out faint echos of its opposite. Laughter and tears must have accompanied the story-telling, for the events combine the ludicrous and the sublime, freedom and destiny.

A Broken Vow

On one level Samson's real failure relates to his inability to keep the vow of a Nazirite, a pledge, incidentally, that his mother made in his behalf. In connection with his first going down to Timnah and determination to take a Philistine wife, Samson violated the vow implicitly. On his second journey to Timnah he violated the first part of the vow explicitly, for he ate honey "unclean" from contact with a carcass. His participation in the drinking bout associated with the wedding constituted a violation of the second regulation, the prohibition against alcoholic beverages. Finally, the disclosure to Delilah of the divine secret concerning his hair was the "fatal breaking of the vow."[7] The actual violation of the latter vow came while Samson slept on Delilah's knee. The other infractions occurred when Samson knew what he was doing. This one, however, stemmed from another person's actions upon Samson. Curiously, Samson's strength departed only with this latter breach of the vow. One might argue that Samson never violated the vow in regard to drinking strong beverages or touching unclean things, since his strength remained with him. The peripheral role of the vow in the entire saga warns against reaching such a conclusion.[8]

The curious difference between the angel's prophecy about Samson and his mother's quotation of that prophecy may derive from the secondary role of the Nazirite vow. Alternatively, the shorter version may reflect a scrupulous conscience about the veracity of God's messenger. Since Samson betrayed the Nazirite vow, it was an error to claim, as his mother did, that the boy would be a Nazirite from birth to death. Instead, the angel promises only that he will be a Nazirite from birth.

Theological Dimensions of the Story

If it is true that Samson depicts an anti-hero, we have to look elsewhere for the real hero of the story. A clue to this person occurs in the birth narrative, which points beyond the mother or the child yet to be born to the God who gave a foretaste of his wondrous nature. In truth Yahweh stands behind Samson's marvelous victories and seizes him time and again to wreak havoc upon his enemies. The final episode succeeds in focusing all eyes upon the One who heard Samson's prayer and answered it with remarkable swiftness.

In the case of another negative example, Saul, no such positive response came from God. Instead Saul sought God's word in vain, and finally marched courageously into a battle that would prove fatal. Saul's prayer was met with strong silence; Samson's penetrated the heavens. Consequently, Samson's death breaks out of the domain of the tragic, inasmuch as he departs in communion with his God. In this moment we lift our eyes above the rubble and behold divine compassion that made such a sacrifice as Samson's possible and noble. Thus our story comes full circle, and we return to the sense of wonder in the presence of an active God with which it began.

If we are correct in this assessment of the theological dimension of the story, we should be cautious about describing the saga as secular. Perhaps a closer look at the theology reflected in the Samson narrative would supply a corrective against excessive praise of this story's earthy spirit at the expense of its genuine religious tone.

We must distinguish between the theological framework within which the narrative has been placed and the story itself. The former belongs to the familiar theological pragmatism that characterizes the Deuteronomistic history. It assumes that the Lord punished Israel for sins, mostly cultic, and that he used foreign powers as instruments of that punishment. According to this view, Israel continually turned away from the Lord to do evil, almost as if she had an evil disposition. Elsewhere we learn that the Deuteronomistic theology laid great stress upon God's willingness to hear Israel's cry for deliverance. The punishment functioned positively; one could almost speak of a pedagogy of suffering at the hands of hostile neighboring peoples.

Not only does the theology of the framework assume that Israel was an inveterate sinner and that God looked upon her with compassion; it also recognizes that the Lord cannot ignore sin. Evil must be punished, for it constitutes apostasy from the living God. It follows that sinners cannot long prosper, for God will not allow his name to be profaned with impunity.

Furthermore, the introductory verse also implies that Israel makes up a people, God's people. They may belong to separate tribes or clans, and they may even boast of membership in the most prestigious tribe. But in God's sight they constitute a holy people, a chosen group whose mission was to live according to the laws made known to Moses. Consequently, the comprehensive term "children of Israel" appears instead of "the Danites" or "the people of Judah."

We note a temporal expression in the framework, one that implies a limit to the punishment of God's people. According to this expression, the Philistines dominated Israel for two gener-

ations, forty years. Of course this particular view of divine
control of events arose *ex post facto*. Still, it gave assurance to
a later sinful community that God's back would not be turned
forever. In due time he would deliver his people from their
oppressors, for his honor was at stake.

The final framing verse, which also occurs prematurely at
15:20, provides an additional piece of information about the
theology of the redactor who set the framework of the saga.
According to it, Samson judged *Israel* twenty years. We may
quarrel with the desire to bestow such an honor upon one
whose only interest was to repay personal grievances, and
whose activity barely exceeded the territorial limits of his own
clan and Philistine cities. In any event, the narrator viewed
Samson as a judge over Israel. In both terms he was exceedingly generous. Judges normally delivered others than themselves from oppression, and the impact of their activity reached
beyond personal revenge. Others within Israel benefitted
greatly from what they did. On the contrary, no one profited
from Samson's exploits but the mighty Danite, and perhaps
those who enjoyed hearing about his wondrous deeds.

Within the narrative itself the Deuteronomistic theological
position surfaces at one significant point. The exuberant expression of gratitude for victory over Samson accords with similar victory shouts within Israel's sacred literature. The grateful
Philistines praise their god for giving them victory over their
mighty foe. In their view, as in the Deuteronomistic historian's,
victory came as a divine gift. In this instance Dagon gave the
victory; elsewhere the Lord defeated his enemies.

We do not need to appeal to the Mesha stela for authentica-
tion of such sentiment. Of course the Moabites understood defeat at the hands of Israelites as evidence of Chemosh's anger,
and viewed the reversal of their fortunes as a sign of his
renewed favor. We can assume that this understanding of reality characterized most religious peoples, for the connection between virtue and prosperity has plagued religion from its
inception.[9] After all, who can quarrel with a desire to praise
God for success?

If we turn to the Samson stories themselves and characterize their theology, we observe at the outset that a martial spirit
colors everything that is said about the Lord. Even the birth of
Samson falls into these surging waters. Samson will begin to
deliver Israel from the hand of the Philistines. As the lad ma-
tures, Yahweh itches for a fight; he can hardly wait to provoke
a skirmish with the Philistines. His spirit seizes Samson and
wreaks havoc among the enemy. It matters little to him
whether the Timnites, Askelonites or Gazites are innocent victims of Samson's fury. His sole concern is to assure Samson
success against his foes. In short, whatever else we can say
about Yahweh, he was a warrior.[10]

But more can be said, even if it belongs to the underside of
this martial emphasis. God protects his own people and delivers them in adversity. The birth story concerns one area in
which he deigns to set things right. This God hardly enters
human history on his own; instead he sends an envoy to proclaim good tidings and to instruct Manoah and his wife about
special requirements relating to the wondrous son. This messenger's countenance radiated divine majesty, and his conduct
implied special relationship with God. Consequently, the angel
refused to partake of a meal with Manoah. Furthermore, the
angel's wondrous departure in fire suggested to Manoah and
his wife that they had beheld God.

This God delights in ritual purity. Thus he insists that Samson avoid strong drink, impurity, and a razor. That is, ethical
behavior is irrelevant to this God, whose sole interest concerns
external matters. Samson can murder and fornicate, and God
will continue to bless him. But let him cut off his hair, and God
will depart from him forthwith.

Samson's God can be reached in time of distress, even after
betrayal of the vow. Just as he answered Manoah's prayer for
further information, he responded favorably to Samson and
provided water for a thirsty warrior, and, in the end, restored
the blind hero's strength. He may be a warrior God, lacking
ethical perception and overly enthusiastic about ritualistic
matters, but he watches over his own people. Eager to deliver

Israel from the Philistines, he raises up Samson and sustains him in every adversity. Just as he used suffering to teach Israel a vital lesson, he let Samson endure pain, humiliation, and ridicule so that the Danite would learn to rely wholly upon God for strength.

If God is viewed as a warrior whose only interest is to promote the wellbeing of his people, even by means of suffering at the hands of their enemy, how is the human creature understood in the saga? We have already discussed the positive attitude toward Samson's mother, who belongs alongside the ancestor of Israel's faith, Sarah. The beautiful Timnite also soars to lofty heights, in spite of Samson's derogatory epithet for her. Forced by sheer necessity, she wept until Samson disclosed his secret to her. But the betrayal of her husband arose from fear and constituted a desperate attempt to survive at any price. The other two women scarcely deserve such praise. The harlot merely goes about her profession; she fades into oblivion because nothing about her transcends the sensual. Delilah, on the other hand, earned our scorn. Willing to sacrifice love for money, and eager to elevate the Philistine cause, she betrayed one who professed love for her and who put complete faith in her trustworthiness. Curiously, she prospered from her treacherous conduct; like Abraham in Egypt, she emerged from the experience a rich person. Nothing is said of either's ethical impoverishment.

Manoah has been accused of attempting to secure divine power by discovering the sacred name.[11] The divine response to his prayer and the theophany afforded him scarcely support such a thesis, even if Manoah became the target of divine and human rebuke. Before God he prostrated himself, and even allowed his wife to have the last word.

Samson's behavior typifies that of all Israel. Again and again he entered into alliances that placed his sacred trust in jeopardy. In each instance he depended upon the Lord to extricate him from the cesspool into which he threw himself. His actions give the impression of spontaneity, although monologues correct this view of him. The latter glimpses into his thoughts depict him as a reflective soul, one who only wants to be left alone—once he has gotten revenge on his foes.

Samson's religion prompts him to pray for help in desperate straits. Once he uses the venerable self-designation, "thy servant," and approaches self-pity in his request for water. His other prayer bears witness to conviction that God had not forsaken him although all others had. Even the violation of his vow had not driven a wedge between him and God: All things could be set right in a moment. Contrition of heart secured divine compassion. The sinner need not despair so long as Yahweh was his or her God.

To sum up, the framework and saga breathe a deeply religious spirit. While direct points of contact between the two can be observed, the saga manifests its own distinct religiosity. For this reason we reject all attempts to isolate religious expressions in the saga as secondary accretions. Certainly, the Philistines' victory song belongs to the original tale, as does the frequent reference to Yahweh's spirit. Once we have conceded that much, nothing prevents the accepting of the birth narrative as an integral part of the saga, and with it, the recognition story. It follows that God is the real hero of the Samson saga. Judges come and go; they carry out their commission with varying degrees of faithfulness. When true to their calling, they deliver Israel from her oppressor. And when only faithful under extreme circumstances, they *begin* to deliver Israel from the hand of the Philistines. But whatever they do, these judges rely upon the Judge of the whole earth. He alone can deliver Israel once and for all time, for he does not sleep on Delilah's knee.

Neither the theme of a broken vow nor even the conflict between filial devotion and erotic attachment adequately characterizes the Samson saga. Important as they are, these themes point beyond themselves to the mystery of divine compassion for a barren woman and a fallen hero. In doing so, they focus all eyes upon a love that transcends all human relationships, parental or conjugal.

From Saint to Tragic Hero

In the words of the divine messenger, Samson was destined to be a Nazirite from birth and would begin to deliver Israel from the Philistines. This marvelous prediction concerns the lad's personal lifestyle and his public office. As a consequence of the angel's high hopes for this child of promise, both Manoah and his wife expected their son to bring honor upon the family and rest to a weary people. Neither hope materialized; instead, Samson brought disgrace to his family and departed with Philistines still in command of Israelites. In the face of such aborted hope, a redactor put forth an even more audacious claim—that Samson judged Israel for twenty years.

Samson did not even begin to deliver Israel from the Philistines,[12] despite his success in conflict with these uncircumcised foes. On the single occasion when a brother clan had a chance to join him in a valiant attempt to throw off the yoke that had long suppressed the proud inhabitants of Judah, those men chose bondage's security over an uncertain future on the battlefield. On still another occasion, Samson exposed the city of Gaza to attack by transporting its gates to far-away Hebron. We do not hear a word about courageous action to take advantage of the enemy's vulnerability. Similarly, Samson's final act, in which he brought the house down upon the heads of those who came to watch him make sport, seriously weakened Philistine power. Despite this fact, we do not find any allusion to decisive military action that aimed at striking a blow to foreign rule.

As a judge over Israel, Samson fared little better. Not one of his skirmishes against the enemy fits the pattern we have learned to expect of an Israelite judge.[13] No oppressed people cried out for deliverance, and none benefitted directly from his victories. In every instance Samson's battles were personal vendettas. He slew thirty men of Askelon because an equal number of Timnites had grievously offended him; he killed a thousand Philistines because they had burned his wife and her father; he crushed the Gazites because they had gouged out his eyes. The mere datum that he acted on divine impulse cannot silence these significant facts, however much one may emphasize the claim that the spirit of God seized Samson.

Certain additional features of Samson's behavior accord ill with expectations aroused by the Lord's messenger. Having read about his marvelous birth, and about his deeply religious parents, we expect much more from Samson than murder, fornication and boundless pride. Surely the endowment of God's spirit had some nobler goal than the ambushing of innocent Askelonites, the satisfying of sexual desire in the bed of a harlot, and the arrogant boast that his own hand alone had given him victory over a thousand Philistines. Not once did Samson transcend self-interest, even at the moment of his death.

Naturally, Samson's presence in the Hebrew canon poses something of a problem for some people. As a result, interpreters early formulated a significant question: Was Samson a saint or a tragic hero? We can state the question another way to focus upon the decisive issue: Is Samson valuable solely as a negative example?[14] The struggle to answer this question has enriched the Samson story in many ways. We turn now to an examination of major responses to the above question: Was Samson a saint or a tragic hero?

Samson as a Saint

Ben Sira overlooked Samson in his well-known account of those belonging to Israel's "Hall of Fame" (44:1—49:16), although he did allude to "the judges also, with their respective names" (46:11). In the Epistle to the Hebrews, Samson joins Gideon, Barak, Jephthah, David, Samuel, and unnamed prophets as representatives of faith who accomplished mighty things, but were denied the fulfillment of God's promises that had become accessible to Jesus' followers (11:32–40). The two-fold mention of faith in this brief passage stands out impressively, particularly the testimony that all these persons were well attested by their faith. In some small measure, at least, this text begins to salvage Samson's tainted reputation.

Josephus expanded this salvage operation in another direction. In his view, Samson was a man of extraordinary virtue in all respects except his relationship with women. He wrote: "That he let himself be ensnared by a woman must be imputed to human nature which succumbs to sins; but testimony is due to him for his surpassing excellence in all the rest."[15] Josephus was particularly impressed by Samson's courage as manifested in his dying moment, for he had himself broken a solemn pact to commit suicide rather than surrender to Roman soldiers.

Samson's brief visit to a Gazite harlot does not appear in Josephus' account. Instead, we read that Samson lodged at an inn. Conceivably, Josephus was acquainted with a variant tradition, for he did not hesitate to label Delilah a harlot. It follows that the silence about a harlot from Gaza did not arise from a desire to exonerate Samson. In reality, Josephus conceded that Samson transgressed the laws of God, altered his way of living, and initiated strange foreign customs into Israelite life.

One means of elevating Samson does occur in Josephus' account, namely the exaltation of his parents. Josephus described Manoah as a Danite who possessed great virtue, indeed he called him the chief person of his country. According to Josephus, Manoah's wife was equally outstanding; her widely celebrated beauty provoked her husband to jealousy. The enthusiasm with which she reported the story of the messenger's appearance to her, and her emphasis upon his youth and good looks, inflamed Manoah's ever-smouldering jealousy. His behavior prompted *her* to pray that the messenger return to clear up the matter and remove her husband's suspicions that she may have engaged in unseemly conduct.

In short, Josephus sought to honor Samson for extraordinary virtue in spite of certain evidence of weakness. In addition, he embellished the biblical story in several details, particularly those concerning Samson's parents. Still, Josephus found the scandalous stories of Samson's liaisons with foreign women well-established, and made the most of their presence by reminding readers of human nature.

Largely on the basis of Samson's striking presence in the list of faithful persons in Hebrews, early Christian interpreters began to view him as a saint.[16] By the fourth century

Athanasius linked him with David and Samuel as saintly persons (ágioi). Augustine wrote of Moses, Daniel and Samson as our fathers (patres nostri) who rose up against false gods, and argued that the latter's suicide did not alter the fact of his sainthood. In a word, Samson was resplendent in repentance.

One way of maintaining Samson's place among the saints was to view his fall as divinely planned. Theodoret, for example, wrote that God allowed Samson's fall for his own greater purposes. The precise reasons for the Nazirite's betrayal of his vow and subsequent dishonor varied with the interpreter. Josephus listed four reasons for Samson's fall: (1) he was allured by a woman; (2) he was only human; (3) he sought conformity with Gentile fashions; and (4) he succumbed to hybris. Gregory the Great also emphasized Samson's pride, whereas Jerome thought Samson's lust was the real reason for his downfall.

Similarities between Samson and Hercules struck interpreters from the outset. Both demonstrated strength greater than that of the king of the beasts; both were ruined by women; both chose death voluntarily; and both performed remarkable feats of strength. Comparison with Hercules tended to confirm the view of Samson as an extraordinary person. Saintliness was the Christian means of expressing this conviction.

Samson's repentance strengthened the case for spiritual exaltation. To be sure, he betrayed his special calling and suffered the consequences of his irresponsible conduct. But he did not remain a victim of perfidy; instead he recognized his need for divine assistance and called upon the Lord. Laying aside his former pride, Samson pleaded that God remember him once more.

Surely the most striking exaltation of Samson was a tendency to view him as a type of Christ. Encouraged by allegorical interpretation of the Samson saga, Rupert of St. Heribert (12th c.) contended that Samson was a type of Christ in at least these ways: (1) he performed seven wondrous feats, as there are seven sacraments; (2) the blinding of Samson represents the agony of Christ; and (3) Samson's death by the pillars supporting the Philistine house prefigured Christ's death on the cross. Much

earlier, Ambrose had interpreted Samson's locks as a prefigur-
ing of Christ, and Augustine had preached sermons on Samson
in which he described the incident at Gaza as a type of Christ's
harrowing of hell.

A publication in the seventeenth century lay down nine
ways in which Samson resembled Christ:

1. the births of both were foretold by a heavenly messenger
   and were marvelous in character;
2. Samson freed oppressed Israelites from the Philistines,
   and Jesus liberated Jews from Satan's power;
3. Samson slew a lion, and Jesus conquered Satan, who
   walks about like a roaring lion;
4. the spirit departed from Samson and let him fall; God
   permitted Christ's spirit to depart so that he could die;
5. both Samson and Jesus fought their battles without the
   aid of companions;
6. for a bribe Delilah betrayed Samson with kisses; having
   accepted a bribe, Judas planted a kiss on Jesus' cheek;
7. Israelites bound Samson with cords that could not contain
   him, and Jews bound Jesus who could not be held by
   Roman soldiers or death itself;
8. at Gaza Samson escaped from an ambush and carried off
   the city gates; Jesus arose from the grave which was
   guarded by Roman soldiers;
9. God's spirit permitted Samson's death and the resultant
   slaughter of Philistines; Jesus was slain, but left Jews and
   Romans desolate.[17]

Strong reaction set in among certain critics, who viewed
Samson as a figure of the antichrist. These interpreters focused
upon Samson as whoremonger, murderer, and selfish warrior.
In their view, Samson scarcely exemplified virtues appropriate
to sainthood. Surely one who had prevailed over a lion could
have conquered his passions if he had wished. In addition, Samson's slaughtering of innocent people did not fall into the category of necessary self-defense during battle. Furthermore, his
proud arrogance following victory over a thousand Philistines

seemed inappropriate for one of such high calling, particularly since God's spirit made the victory possible.

To summarize, Samson's conduct notwithstanding, he was honored by Christian interpreters as a saint. Not only that, his life was viewed over against Jesus', and many similarities led to an understanding of Samson as a type of Christ. It mattered little ultimately that he squandered his energies with harlots and died at his own hands. In the final resort, he called upon God for help, thus returning at last to his original calling as deliverer of Israel.

Samson as a Tragic Hero

At the same time, Christian interpreters recognized the powerful negative example contained within the story of Samson. His frequent sexual encounters furnished vivid examples of the dangers inherent within such license. An inability to master his sexual appetite led to Samson's loss of freedom, betrayal of his vocation, and forfeiture of life. Clement of Rome made Samson an *a fortiori* example in arguing for chastity. He wrote of Samson as one "whom a woman brought to ruin with her wretched body, and her vile passion."[18] Turning to his audience, Clement asked: "Art thou, perchance, such a man as he?" and warned: "Know thyself, and know the measure of thy strength."

Actually, only the final episode communicates unambiguously this warning against sexual excesses. As for the experience with the lovely Timnite, we can not accuse Samson of lechery inasmuch as, at Samson's insistence, Manoah arranged a marriage between his son and the beautiful maiden. It was not Samson's fault that the plans went awry. Nor can we consider Samson's brief visit of a harlot a clear warning that sexual license inevitably leads to one's ruin. On the contrary, Samson emerged from that encounter unscathed. Not only that, he walked away with the gates to the city on his shoulders. The Delilah incident does warn against free association with a woman, although any conclusion about sexual relations between the two is inferential. We are only told that Samson loved her—and slept on her knees. Still, the story implies more than it actually articulates, so that we probably do not go astray in understanding their relationship as erotic.

Some critics felt the force of this narrative so fully that they endeavored to remove any hint of sexual misconduct on Samson's part. Certain rationalist thinkers claimed that at Gaza Samson lodged in the house of a woman "that sold vittayles," although this language may represent a clever double entendre. Still others debated Delilah's status, some viewing her as Samson's wife and others thinking of her as his concubine. Alfonsus Tostadus' commentaries on the Heptateuch carried through a rationalistic approach to the entire Samson story. He raised certain questions about the narrative itself. For example, he asked: Why did the guards at Gaza not see Samson when he emerged from the harlot's quarters; why did the Philistines not slay Samson while he slept on Delilah's knees; why did Samson always fall in love with Philistine women; how did Samson's brothers recognize his body among all the slain people of Gaza?

Nevertheless, certain features of Samson's conduct could hardly be condoned. Few critics felt that Samson should act as a model for others, particularly in three areas: killing, lechery, and pride. Some interpreters exercised considerable liberty in discovering negative examples within the Samson story. Perhaps the most ingenious effort in this regard is that by Richard Rogers, who claimed that Samson's loss of his hair warns Christians against preening themselves.[19]

One consequence of viewing Samson as a negative hero was a tendency to describe him in tragic categories. As we have seen, several ingredients of tragedy mark the Samson saga: a propensity toward forming alliances with foreign women; betrayal by one he loved; and, of course, suicide. Himself something of a tragic figure, Peter Abelard wrote a poem about Samson as a tragic character. This interpretation took critics by storm, and the story became secularized bit by bit. Chaucer's monk gave more space to Samson than to Lucifer, Adam, or Hercules. The same was true of Chaucer's predecessor, Boccaccio, who blamed Delilah for Samson's misfortune.

But I dar calle hir Dalida the double,
Cheeff roote & cause off al his mortal trouble.[20]

This emphasis upon Samson as a tragic victim of divine purpose and his own inherent weakness of character shifted the
focus to the final episode of the Samson saga. The Delilah incident and its sequel, which alone had been introduced into the
Christian liturgy during the seventh century, readily lent itself
to a tragic reading. In some works, all religious elements of the
story were removed, and the story was rewritten. *Cursor Mundi*
(14th c.), for example, has Delilah remarry, and Samson dies at
her wedding feast.

In short, Samson had traveled a long journey from saint to
tragic hero by the time John Milton chose him as the subject
for his epic treatment of primary temptation. During Milton's
day another significant shift in the nature of Samson's tragedy
took place. This change placed emphasis upon Samson's failure
in high calling, and thus stressed the tragedy of his spiritual
suffering. In Milton's tragedy, Samson symbolized every person's struggle against evil and its temptation, in whatever
form. Significantly, Samson won in this contest, for he with-
stood temptation. Thus he took a giant stride toward sainthood
once again.

Milton's Samson Agonistes

Inasmuch as Milton's portrayal of Samson brings together
the several understandings that we have just described, and
subsumes them under a powerful psychological analysis of suffering, a brief look at the major characteristics of this tragedy
seems appropriate. We shall give special attention to character
development in the poem, hoping to ascertain Milton's enrich-
ment of Samson's character from what he found in the biblical
account.

The plot of *Samson Agonistes* is simple. While the captive
Samson rests from his labors on a festival day, certain Danites
(the chorus) visit him to bring a measure of comfort. Later
Manoah arrives and informs his son that he hopes to secure
Samson's ransom from the Philistines. In passing, he informs
Samson that the captors are celebrating a thanksgiving feast

to Dagon for victory over Samson. While Manoah begins to carry out his hoped-for transaction to secure his son's freedom, Samson receives two visitors who seek to determine his general state before the Philistine lords dare invite him to do sport in their midst. The first is Delilah, Samson's wife. She begs his forgiveness, and offers various excuses for her action that brought about his present ignominy. Unmoved by her honied words, Samson at last provokes her to confess that she eagerly anticipates honors from her countrymen. The second visitor is Harapha, a Philistine giant, who freely insults Samson; the latter challenges him three times to combat, but the cowardly Philistine champion slips away in much distress. Samson's moral courage now equals his physical strength. A third visitor summons Samson to the festival at Gaza; after refusing at first, Samson perceives that this is God's doing, and accompanies the public officer, who has by now retraced his steps to repeat the summons. About this time Manoah returns, full of hope that for a price he can persuade the Philistines to set Samson free. A great uproar reaches his ears, and with his countrymen he awaits news of what has happened in Gaza. At last a messenger brings the tragic word, and Manoah discovers that his son has died heroically.

We notice at first glance that Milton has taken certain liberties with the biblical story. The major differences in plot concern Manoah and Delilah, as well as the introduction of a new character, Harapha. Although the Bible remains silent about Manoah in the Delilah episode and its sequel, Milton introduces a marvelous leitmotif that brings the aged father into direct contact with his fallen son. This permits father and son to discuss issues as trivial as family pride and as profound as divine justice. Both Samson and Manoah are fully aware of the irony involved in the reversal of relationships forced upon the two men: The aged father envisions caring for his son when it should be the other way around. Both also recognize the contrast between what Samson once was and his fallen state. But the father's love for his son impels him to extreme measures; he will stop at nothing to secure Samson's freedom. He is prepared, in short, to *beg* hated Philistines, and to spend every cent of his patrimony:

> . . . much rather I shall chuse
> To live the poorest in my Tribe, then richest,
> And he in that calamitous prison left. . . .
> Not wanting him, I shall want nothing (1478–80, 1484).

Such affection for his wondrous son leads Manoah to question God's fairness. He cannot understand why God punished Samson for a single error, when his positive deeds were multiple. Such dark thoughts are accompanied by radical questioning of the wisdom of praying for good things.

> . . . Nay what thing good
> Pray'd for, but often proves our woe, our bane? . . .
> Why are his gifts desirable, to tempt
> Our earnest Prayers, then giv'n with solemn hand
> As Graces, draw a Scorpion's tail behind? (350–51, 358–360)

From this depiction of the aged Manoah, it is perfectly clear that in Milton's eyes suffering was not limited to Samson.

In *Samson Agonistes* Delilah is Samson's wife, whereas she was his mistress in the biblical story. The reason for this difference resides in legal statutes, not moral custom.[21] A wife's first duty is to her husband. Neither State nor Religion has prior claim upon Delilah's devotion, for she owes supreme loyalty to Samson. By this slight shift in her status from mistress to wife, Milton divested Delilah of any justifiable reason for her treachery. Although she claimed that her actions arose from allegiance to the State, and simultaneously to God, Samson was able to dispute that argument by reminding her of a wife's first duty.

The change from mistress to wife signifies far greater differences in Milton's Delilah and the biblical character. Perhaps the reasons she advances for her treacherous behavior best suggest the way he enriched Delilah's personality. She first appeals to woman's natural curiosity and weakness, and follows that argument with the claim that she acted to keep him at home with her lest his venturesome spirit and roving eye impel him to new surroundings. In seeking his forgiveness, she reminds Samson that he first showed her the way to divulge secret knowledge. In addition, Delilah pleads with Samson to let her negotiate his release in her custody. Having fallen into her hands when he possessed his great strength, Samson is not about to surrender himself to her care now that he has no defenses against abuse, which he feels certain will follow. In desperation, she plays her trump card—the appeal to physical beauty. This ploy, too, fails, and Samson refuses to let her touch him at all. In one sense, she does touch Samson as neither his father nor his friends are able to do: "Samson literally and physically springs to his feet as he hears her name."[22] In the end, she "brought him to life, made him conscious of his manhood."[23]

Milton introduced a wholly new character into the plot. A Philistine giant, Harapha, visits the captive Samson and taunts him. The contrast between the two figures is noteworthy. The mighty Philistine warrior, eager for a chance to demonstrate his prowess in combat with the infamous Israelite judge, informs Samson that the story would have been different if he had been present when Samson used an ass's jawbone as a weapon. The Philistine accuses Samson of murder, revolt, and theft. By now Samson has regained his strength, if not his sight, and puts the boastful, but cowardly, Harapha to flight.

We have thus arrived at the real difference between Milton's *Samson Agonistes* and the biblical story. "In Milton's hands he (Samson) comes alive as an intensely suffering human being, struggling with God, struggling with himself—much more like Job than the legendary giant of Judges. The Bible emphasizes his strength; Milton his psychology."[24] One could even say that *Samson Agonistes* "is preeminently a psychological study of the development of a human being."[25] Samson refuses to blame God for his own folly. Instead, he assumes full responsibility for his actions, and laments most of all the religious implications of his conduct. His agony mounts, therefore, when he learns that his defeat exalts Dagon among the Gazites. Ultimately, he realizes that the real struggle is not between him and the Philistines, but between Yahweh and Dagon.

Such a spiritual struggle accomplishes catharsis for those who join hands with Samson in his awful ordeal. Robbed of an inkling of suspense, since we know the outcome of the story, "we feel the emotions of pity and fear, so that we involve ourselves with the character, suffering in his suffering, experiencing intense pity for him."[26] With Samson we achieve a heroic, though tragic, victory over primal temptation.

This Samson differs from the biblical one in reflective capacity, which permits him no rest even when his body finds ease. He knows by intuition that God prompted his marital alliances, and rejoices that he assists God in carrying out his purposes. He even recognizes the possibility that God would work something extraordinary in Samson's last hour, although without nullifying Samson's Nazirite status. He remarks:

> This day will be remarkable in my life
> By some great act, or of my days the last (1388–1389).

That remarkable feat set the tragic hero free once and for all.

> . . . but death who sets all free
> Hath paid his ransom now and full discharge (1572–1573).

In one particular, at least, *Samson Agonistes* becomes palpably autobiographical for Milton. Samson's blindness was a malady that Milton understood as few others could have done. One cannot miss the overwhelming pathos filling speech after speech in which Samson describes and laments his awful, dark torment.

> . . . but chief of all,
> O loss of sight, of thee I must complain!
> Blind among enemies, O worse than chains,
> Dungeon, or beggery, or decrepit age! (66–69)

> O dark, dark, dark, amid the blaze of noon,[27]
> Irrecoverably dark, total Eclipse
> Without all hope of day! (80–82)

> Which shall I first bewail,
> Thy bondage or lost Sight,

Prison within Prison
Inseparably dark?
Thou art become (O worst imprisonment!)
The Dungeon of thy self. . . . (151–156)

In truth, Samson affords Milton an occasion to wrestle with his own blindness within a tragic setting. Regretting the dire consequences of his folly, Samson envisions a context in which the God of Israel puts Dagon to shame. In that confrontation, Samson played no small role despite his blindness. In the end, saint and tragic hero was "overstrong" against himself.

Afterword: The Secret Is Out

The Samson saga demonstrates Israelite narrative art at its zenith. It arose in a heroic age, a time when Danites engaged in "unrestricted intercourse, *connubium* and *commercium*"[1] and gravitated toward Philistine cities. Such an era was geared to war; it boasted "plenty of sport and horse-play, feasting and wining and not a little bawdy."[2] Most of all, it thrilled to love stories. Not a few wars grew out of amorous adventures from Shechem to the valley of Sorek and beyond those regions.

Such tales of erotic quests and their devastating consequences developed through free adaptation of literary conventions. Formulaic expressions, motifs, and rhetorical devices bore eloquent testimony to the skill of numerous poets and narrators. Many different types of literature contributed to the effective transmission of heroic exploits: prayers, aetiologies, victory songs, riddles, heroic deed, birth story, recognition story. Although earthy from the outset, the Samson saga also bore witness to the source of superhuman strength, particularly through reference to the spirit of Yahweh.

Certain important motifs link the Samson saga with kindred texts within Israel's literary corpus. These portray a barren wife, a mighty hero meeting his nemesis in a woman, a quest for a deity's secret name, a death wish, loss of charisma, and terror over theophany. An author, or several perceptive writers, freely drew upon the full range of stylistic devices that constituted *belles lettres* in ancient Israel.

In addition, the author chose a unifying theme, the choice between filial devotion and erotic attachment, that gave the stories unity and audience appeal. His treatment of this highly explosive issue demonstrated sensitivity and conviction. Although opting for marriage within the ranks of the Danite clan, the author conceded the great attraction Israelites felt for Philistines. Positive reaction to this lure could only result in calamity, despite the pleasurable moments.

Heroes in this exciting age were not simpletons. Capable of considerable skill at repartee, Samson sought to impress Philistines with his wit. To do so, he chose the appropriate means— a riddle contest. Essentially a test of worth, this exercise in futility succeeded only in blighting the budding relationship between Samson and his wife. Both Samson and his opponents had mastered the art of riddling, and the latter excelled at devious conduct as well.

The story combines tragic and comic elements with tremendous effect. Samson's *penchant* for foreign women drove him closer and closer to dark death, until at last he led an innocent lad into the same darkness. The lovely Timnite bride labored valiantly to escape a fiery death; eventually she fell victim to her own people's fury. Innocent Askelonites died at the hands of an angry Samson, whom they had neither befriended nor offended. But ludicrous episodes also occur, and thus prevent the taking of the saga too seriously. Still, tragic and comic elements give way before a stronger impulse—a tendency to lift one's eyes toward the heavens.

The Samson saga explores certain ambiguities of reality. It refuses to offer simple solutions for complex problems like endogamy and exogamy, human freedom and divine destiny, eros and charisma. Instead, the story depicts life as it transpired. As a result, Samson is neither saint nor sinner. Early Christian scholars labored much to turn him into a saint, despite his amorous conduct, violent personality, and suicide. In time he became a tragic hero, secular once again, but endowed with considerably more reflective powers. John Milton advanced the tradition even more; in *Samson Agonistes* the hero waged heroic warfare against temptation and triumphed in his final act.

Truly, the biblical saga entertains and instructs. With remarkable power, it brings to life the exciting story of one who recognized "no higher guide than his own wayward passions,"[3] despite his unusual origin. But entertainment does not suffice; the saga also teaches the Israelites about One who performs wonders, even when human subjects squander their talents and calling. By telling and re-telling this marvelous story of Samson and his loves, those who found themselves in trying circumstances discovered renewed hope.[4] Thus they proclaimed the greatest secret of all: God heeds the cry of those who recognize their own helplessness. Like Samson of old, Israel frequently found herself in need of divine remembrance, and joined the ancient hero in a single request. "Remember me, O Lord." She did so at great risk. Failure to raise her voice for remembrance carried even greater risk.

Abbreviations

AB	Anchor Bible
ANET . .	James B. Pritchard, ed. *Ancient Near Eastern Texts: Relating to the Old Testament*. 3rd Edition with supplement (Princeton: University Press, 1969).
ATD. . . .	Das Alte Testament Deutsch
BBB. . . .	Bonner Biblische Beiträge
Bib	Biblica
BZAW . .	Beihefte zur Zeitschrift für die alttestamentliche Wissenschaft
CB.	Century Bible
Ency Jud.	Encyclopedia Judaica
EvQ. . . .	Evangelical Quarterly
HKAT . .	Hand-Kommentar zum Alten Testament
HUCA . .	Hebrew Union College Annual
IB	Interpreters' Bible
ICC	International Critical Commentary
IDB	Interpreters' Dictionary of the Bible
Inter . . .	Interpretation: A Journal of Bible and Theology
JAAR. . .	Journal of the American Academy of Religion
JBL	Journal of Biblical Literature
JQR. . . .	Jewish Quarterly Review
JNES . . .	Journal of Near Eastern Studies
JTS	Journal of Theological Studies
KB	Ludwig Koehler and Walter Baumgartner, *Lexicon in Veteris Testamenti Libros* (Leiden: E. J. Brill, 1958; 3rd Edition, 1967, 1974)
KHCAT .	Kurzer Hand-commentar zum Alten Testament
OTWSA .	Die O. T. Wekgemeenskap in Suid Afrika
RGG . . .	Die Religion in Geschichte und Gegenwart
RHP . . .	Revue d' Histoire et de Philosophie religieuses
RHR . . .	Revue de l'Histoire des Religions
SAT. . . .	Schriften Altes Testament
SBTh . . .	Studies in Biblical Theology
Sem. . . .	Semitics
ThT	Theologisch Tijidschrift
TUMSR .	Trinity University Monograph Series in Religion
UTB. . . .	Uni Taschenbücher
VT	Vetus Testamentum
VTS. . . .	Vetus Testamentum Supplements
WMANT .	Wissenschaftliche Monographien zum Alten und Neuen Testaments
ZAW . . .	Zeitschrift für die alttestamentliche Wissenschaft
ZDA. . . .	Zeitschrift für die Deutsches Alterthum
ZDMG . .	Zeitschrift der Deutschen Morgenlandischen Gesellschaft
ZS	Zeitschrift für Sexualwissenschaft
ZVV . . .	Zeitschrift des Vereins für Volkskunde

Notes*

Introduction

1. This tabulation of proper names omits the divine name, Yahweh, together with the epithet alluded to by God's envoy.

2. H. Steinthal, "The Legend of Samson," in *Mythology Among the Hebrews,* by Ignaz Goldziher (New York: Cooper Square Publishers, 1967), 392–446 (original publication, 1877); Paul Carus, *The Story of Samson* (Chicago: Open Court Publishing Co., 1907).

3. Carus, *The Story of Samson,* 91–92.

4. *Festi,* IV, 679–680.

5. George Foote Moore, *A Critical and Exegetical Commentary on Judges* (ICC; Edinburgh: T. & T. Clark, 1895), 365.

6. Gustav Roskoff, *Die Simsonssage nach ihrer Entstehung, Form und Bedeutung und der Heraclesmythus* (Leipzig: Ernst Bredt, 1860).

7. Roskoff, *Die Simsonssage nach ihrer Entstehung, Form und Bedeutung und der Heraclesmythus,* 22–30, lists the following feats: (1) the slaying of a lion; (2) the proposing of a riddle and subsequent slaughter of thirty men; (3) the catching and setting fire to three hundred foxes; (4) the retaliation for the death of Samson's wife and father-in-law's entire family; (5) the snapping of ropes that bound Samson; (6) the slaughter of a thousand Philistines with the jawbone of an ass; (7) Samson's prayer and miraculous water source; (8) the carrying off of the two doors from Gaza; (9) Samson's breaking of seven new bowstrings; (10) his snapping of seven new ropes; (11) his pulling up of the loom with the web; (12) Samson's pulling down of the two pillars holding up the house of his enemies in Gaza.

8. F. Michael Krouse, *Milton's Samson and the Christian Tradition* (Princeton: University Press, 1949), 44.

9. G.C. Cohen, "Samson and Hercules," *EvQ,* 42 (1970), 131–141 (with much special pleading for the originality of the biblical story).

10. Hermann Gunkel, "Simson," in *Reden und Aufsätze* (Göttingen: Vandenhoeck & Ruprecht, 1913), 38–64.

11. *ANET,* 73–78.

*Abbreviations used in these notes are listed on page 152.

12. Israel's great king who finally conquered the Philistines also confronted his foe with seemingly inferior weaponry—a shepherd's sling. This epic confrontation between David and Goliath can be viewed as an encounter between natural man and cultural man, but such a reading of the story is forced.

13. George W. Shaw, "Shemesh and Samson," *The Monist*, January, 1907, wrote: "His main trait was an irresistible *penchant* for the daughters of the Philistines. He was simply a stout, sensual man, with some humor and shrewdness, but of small mental calibre."

14. Gunkel, "Simson," 41. The narrative implies that the unfortunate inhabitants of Askelon from whom Samson stole thirty garments were dressed in the requisite fine clothing so that Samson paid his debt in full.

15. *KB*, 537. 1 Chronicles 2:52–54 refers to Manahathites, and leads some interpreters to think a *heros eponymous* of the Danite clan was later identified as Samson's father.

16. *KB*, 210 (amorous behavior). A. Vincent derives the name from an Arabic root that permits a pun: *"dalla,* to behave amorously, and *dalila,* a guide, here a guide to disaster." For this information, I am indebted to John L. McKenzie, *The World of the Judges* (Englewood Cliffs: Prentice Hall, 1966), 155.

17. For my earlier discussion of the story of Samson, see "The Samson Saga: Filial Devotion or Erotic Attachment?," *ZAW,* 86 (1974), 470–504.

18. Aleida G. van Daalen, *Simson* (Assen: Van Gorcum & Comp., 1966), emphasizes the well-developed plan of salvation history as the unifying feature of the Samson saga.

19. Extensive bibliography appears in Jo Cheryl Exum's 1976 Yale Ph.D. dissertation entitled "Literary Patterns in the Samson Saga: An Investigation of Rhetorical Style in Biblical Prose." I am grateful to Professor Exum for making her study available to me. Although I had already completed my research for the most part, I have profited from her insights gained through rhetorical analysis.

20. We shall be content with only a few examples: (A) drama: Voltaire's five act opera (1733); William Blake's poem (1783); Frank Wedekind, *Simson oder Scham und Eifersucht* (1914); Leonid Nikolayevich, *Samson in Chains* (1923); Henry Bernstein, *Samson* (1907); Vladimir Jabotinsky, *Samson the Nazirite* (1930); Felix Salten, *Samson and Delilah* (1931); (B) art: Rembrandt, Samson's wedding; Samson threatening his father-in-law; Tintoretto; Lucas Cranach, Samson asleep on Delilah's lap; Rubens; Van Dyck; Jacob Steinhardt (erotic woodcut); (C) music: Handel's oratorio, *Samson* (1944); Camille Saint-Saëns, *Samson et Dalila* (1877); Rubin Goldmark, *Samson* (1913); Nicholas Nabokov, incidental music to *Samson Agonistes* (1938). For further details, consult "Samson," *Ency Jud,* 774–777. In addition, see R. Hermann, *Die*

Gestalt Simons bei Luther (Berlin, 1952), K. Gerlach, *Der Simsonstoff in Drama* (1929), and W. Kirkconnell, *Invincible Samson* (1964).

21. I have no desire to inaugurate a new kind of criticism to replace the many approaches available to biblical critics, on which see Georg Fohrer et al., *Exegese des Alten Testaments* (UTB; Heidelberg: Quelle und Meyer, 1973). Although I consider myself a literary critic, I have avoided that term because of its confusion with source criticism. In addition, my approach differs in important details from literary criticism as it is practiced by David A. Robertson, although in many respects we ask comparable questions and attempt to answer them in a similar manner (*The Old Testament and the Literary Critic* [Philadelphia: Fortress Press, 1977]). Still I prefer the term "aesthetic criticism" as the most appropriate description of what I strive to achieve —an appreciation for the craft of a story or poem, as well as aesthetic enjoyment of the beauty inherent in words "fitly spoken." In short, aesthetic criticism studies a story or a poem as a work of art.

22. W.K. Wimsatt, Jr. and M.C. Beardsley, "The Intentional Fallacy," in *The Verbal Icon: Studies in the Meaning of Poetry* (Lexington: University of Kentucky Press, 1954), 2–18.

23. Erich Auerbach, *Mimesis: The Representation of Reality in Western Literature* (Princeton: University Press, 1953), 3–23; James L. Crenshaw, "Journey into Oblivion: A Structural Analysis of Genesis 22:1–19," *Soundings,* 58 (1975), 243–256; Luis Alonso-Schökel, "Narrative Structures in the Book of Judith," *Colloquy* 2 (Berkeley: Center for Hermeneutical Studies), 1975; D.F. Rauber, "Literary Values in the Bible: The Book of Ruth," *JBL,* 89 (1970), 27–37; Phyllis Trible, "Two Women in a Man's World: A Reading of the Book of Ruth," *Soundings,* 59 (1976), 251–279.

24. "Three-quarters of our study must always be the attempt to reacquire the traditional content of the imagination" (Renwick and Orton, *The Beginnings of English Literature* (New York: Somerset, 1940), 24.

25. *Fear and Trembling: The Sickness Unto Death* (New York: Anchor Books, 1941), 26–29 especially.

26. The Samson story poses a special problem in this regard in that it departs sharply from the road traveled by most authors of biblical literature. Paul Carus, *The Story of Samson,* 113, sums up the usual attitude of critics well: "The story of Samson is neither refined nor moral, so that even orthodox people will have to confess that it is out of harmony with the general tenor of Biblical traditions." But even where the saga does accord with customary biblical sentiment, it constitutes a major problem. Heads roll, commitments falter, eros prevails, hatred abounds. In addition, cruelty to animals and betrayal of "brother" and husband hardly commend Samson or his acquaintances as nominees for good conduct awards. We must guard against judging

Samson and the others by standards appropriate to our time. Whatever else he may have been, Samson was a child of his own era.

27. For discussion, see my contribution to *Tradition and Theology in the Old Testament*, edited by Douglas A. Knight (Philadelphia: Fortress Press, 1977), 235–258. The essay, "The Human Dilemma and Literature of Dissent," represents a long-standing interest in theodicy, for which see my "Popular Questioning of the Justice of God in Ancient Israel," *ZAW*, 82 (1970), 380–395; idem, "The Problem of Theodicy in Sirach," *JBL*, 94 (1975), 47–64; idem, *Prophetic Conflict* (BZAW, 124; Berlin: Walter de Gruyter, 1971), 23–38; idem, *Studies in Ancient Israelite Wisdom* (New York: KTAV, 1977), 26–35; 43–45; and idem, "Theodicy," *IDB*, Sup (1976), 895–896.

Chapter One
Literary and Stylistic Traditions

1. Walter Harrelson, "The Significance of 'Last Words' for Intertestamental Ethics," *Essays in Old Testament Ethics*, edited by James L. Crenshaw and John T. Willis (New York: KTAV, 1974), 203–213; Hans Walter Wolff, *Anthropology of the Old Testament* (Philadelphia: Fortress, 1974), 99 ("Throughout, the biblical narrators report men's departing words with much more attention than the act of dying").

2. Walter Brueggemann, *The Land* (Philadelphia: Fortress Press, 1977).

3. On the significance of blessing in the Old Testament, see above all Johannes Pedersen, *Israel*, I-II (London: Geoffrey Cumberlege, 1926), 182–212.

4. Douglas A. Knight, *Rediscovering the Traditions of Israel* (Missoula: Society of Biblical Literature), 1973, provides a comprehensive discussion of recent research into ancient Israel's traditions.

5. Shalom Carmy, "The Sphinx as Leader: A Reading of Judges 13–16," *Tradition*, 14, No. 3 (1974), 71, writes: "Samson is in love with a culture he abhors. He desires to live among those alien to him, among whom he can never belong. He *is* the difficult, torturing riddles he invents." Elsewhere Carmy refers to a "combination of resentment towards Philistine superiority and lust for the Philistine's daughter" (72).

6. On prayer in historical narratives, see Jack W. Corvin's Ph.D. dissertation entitled "A Stylistic and Functional Study of the Prose Prayers in the Historical Narratives of the Old Testament" (Emory, 1972), published on demand by University Microfilms Ltd., High Wycomb, England.

7. J.J. Glück, "Paronomasia in Biblical Literature," *Sem*, 1 (1970), 50–78, presents some interesting examples of paronomasia, and supplies further bibliography.

8. G.H. Parke-Taylor, *Yahweh: The Divine Name in the Bible* (Waterloo, Ontario: Wilfrid Laurier University Press, 1975).

9. J. Coert Rylaarsdam, "Nazirite," *IDB*, 3, 526–527.

10. "The Lord (Yahu) is salvation."

11. 1 Samuel 31:4 uses the word *hith'al^elu*, whereas the Samson narrative employs the roots *sachaq* and *tsachaq* (Judges 16:25).

12. On the role of the spirit in Judges, see Georges Auzou, *La force de l'esprit* (Paris: Éditions de l'orante), 1966.

13. "And his prayer triumphs over the twisted climate of his soul; the prayer survives the man" (Carmy, "The Sphinx as Leader: A Reading of Judges 13—16), 76. Carmy remarks on the "childish and immature" quality, indeed the "banality," of Samson's prayer life, but notes that boldness accompanied the immaturity (74).

14. The same verb occurs in the *summoning* of Samson to make sport and in Samson's *cry* to God *(qara')*.

15. *KB*, 748–749.

16. The Latin Vulgate, Syriac, and Old Latin (Codex Lugdunensis).

17. For recent discussion of terminology, see Burke O. Long, *The Problem of Etiological Narrative in the Old Testament* (BZAW, 108: Berlin: A Töpelmann, 1968).

18. Brevard S. Childs, "A Study of the Formula, 'Until this Day,' " *JBL*, 82 (1963), 279–292.

19. Attempts to reproduce the puns in English have not been successful. George Foote Moore renders the Hebrew as follows: "With the jaw-bone of an *ass* I *ass*ailed my *ass*ailants, with the jaw-bone of an *ass* have I slain a thousand men" *(Polychrome Bible)* in Paul Carus, *The Story of Samson* (Chicago: Open Court Publishing Co., 1907), 102. Carus suggests a more literal translation: "With the jaw-bone of an *ass* I'm m*ass*ing them in m*ass*es."

20. On riddles, see my article, "Riddle," in *IDB*, Sup (1976), 749–750; idem, "Wisdom," in *Old Testament Form Criticism* (TUMSR, 2; San Antonio: Trinity University Press, 1974), 225–264, particularly 239–245; idem, "The Samson Saga: Filial Devotion or Erotic Attachment?," *ZAW*, 86 (1974), 488–496 especially.

21. Karl Budde, "Samson," *Hastings' Dictionary of the Bible* (New York: Charles Scribner's Sons, 1902), IV, 377–381, uses the expression "lion of the village."

22. For the ancient Near Eastern background, see A. van Selms, "The Best Man and Bride—from Sumer to St. John with a New Interpretation of Judges, Chapters 14 and 15," *JNES*, 9 (1950), 65–75.

23. Attempts to make Samson's feat more credible by identifying Hebron with a nearby site ignore the fantastic character of the saga, in which the hero easily accomplishes the impossible.

24. R.W. Neff, "The Announcement in Old Testament Birth Stories," Yale Ph.D. dissertation, 1969.

25. For a recent argument of structural unity in this literary complex, see Dennis J. McCarthy, "The Wrath of Yahweh and the Structural Unity of the Deuteronomistic History," Crenshaw and Willis, *Essays in Old Testament Ethics*, 97–110.

26. For elaborate theories of redaction in Judges, see Cuthbert A. Simpson, *Composition of the Book of Judges* (Oxford: Blackwell), 1957 and Otto Eissfeldt, *Die Quellen des Richterbuches* (Leipzig: J.C. Hinrichs'sche Buchhandlung), 1925.

27. On the Philistines, see Benjamin Mazar, "The Philistines and Their Wars with Israel," in *The World History of the Jewish People*, vol. 3, edited by Benjamin Mazar (Tel Aviv: Rutgers University Press, 1971), 164–179; J.C. Greenfield, "Philistines," *IDB*, vol. 3, 791–795.

28. For discussion of that era, see Abraham Malamat, "The Period of the Judges," in *The World History of the Jewish People*, vol. 3, 129–163; John L. McKenzie, *The World of the Judges* (Englewood Cliffs: Prentice-Hall, 1966); A.D.H. Mayes, *Israel in the Period of the Judges* (Naperville, Ill.: A.R. Allenson), 1974; J. Alberto Soggin, *When the Judges Ruled* (London: Lutterworth Press), 1965.

29. According to the arrangement, the wife remained with her family and the husband came to live with her permanently or visited her on occasion. For discussion of marriage in Israel, see O.J. Babb, "Marriage," *IDB*, vol. 3, 278–287.

30. So most commentators.

31. Robert W. Polzin, " 'The Ancestress of Israel in Danger' in Danger," *Semeia*, 3 (Missoula: Scholars Press, 1975), 81–98.

32. Deuteronomy 25:5–10. On Levirate marriage, see Babb, "Marriage," 282–283.

33. Phyllis Trible, "Depatriarchalizing in Biblical Interpretation," *JAAR*, 41 (1973), 30–48.

34. "It is a disgrace to be the father of an undisciplined son, and the birth of a daughter is a loss" (Sirach 22:3).

35. Werner Dommershausen, *Die Estherrolle. Stil und Ziel einer alttestamentlichen Schrift* (Stuttgart: Verlag Katholisches Bibelwerk), 1968.

36. The matchless artistry of this story is brought out by Luis Alonso-Schökel, "Narrative Structures in the Book of Judith," *Colloquy*, 2 (1975) and Toni Craven, "Artistry and Faith in the Book of Judith," *Semeia*, 8 (Missoula: Scholars Press, 1977), 75–101.

37. *ANET*, 12–14.

38. Pedersen, *Israel*, I-II, 245–259.

39. Stanley A. Cook, "The Theophanies of Gideon and Manoah," *JTS*, 28 (1927), 368–383.

40. Robert Boling, *Judges* (AB: Garden City: Doubleday & Company, Inc., 1975), 222.

41. On the death wish, see my contribution to the forthcoming *Isra-*

elite Wisdom: Theological and Literary Essays in Honor of Samuel Terrien, edited by John G. Gammie, Walter A. Brueggemann, W. Lee Humphreys, and James M. Ward (Missoula: Scholars Press, 1977) entitled "The Shadow of Death in Qoheleth," and Gerhard von Rad, "Gerichtsdoxologie," *Schalom: Studien zu Glaube und Geschichte Israels,* edited by Karl-Heinz Bernhardt (Stuttgart: Calwer Verlag, 1971), 28–37.

42. Millar Burrows, "The Literary Category of the Book of Jonah," *Translating and Understanding the Old Testament,* edited by H.T. Frank and W. L. Reed (Nashville: Abingdon, 1970), 80–107, traces recent research into this unusual prophetic book and attempts to identify its type.

43. Carus, *The Story of Samson,* 60, implies that far more lies behind this gift of a kid, which absentee husbands brought to their wives in return for sexual favors (cf. Genesis 38). In the Samson story the erotic connection is clear, but the Tobit narrative has totally erased such an implication if it ever existed.

44. Jörg Jeremias, *Theophanie* (WMANT, 10: Neukirchen-Vluyn: Neukirchener Verlag), 1965, contains a valuable discussion of the biblical notion.

45. Rudolf Otto, *The Idea of the Holy* (New York: Oxford University Press), 1923.

46. One could also mention a preference for cognate accusatives (14:12, 13, 16; 15:8; 16:23, 31) and parataxis.

47. For further discussion of rhetoric, see Wayne C. Booth, *A Rhetoric of Irony* (Chicago and London: University of Chicago Press, 1974); *The Rhetoric of Fiction* (Chicago: University Press, 1961); Robert Scholes, *Elements of Fiction* (New York: Oxford University Press, 1968); R. Scholes and Robert Kellogg, *The Nature of Narrative* (London: Oxford University Press, 1966); Frank Kermode, *The Sense of an Ending* (New York: Oxford University Press, 1967).

48. Martin Noth, "The Background of Judges 17—18," *Israel's Prophetic Heritage: Essays in Honor of James Muilenburg,* edited by Bernhard W. Anderson and Walter Harrelson (New York: Harper & Brothers, 1962), 68–85.

49. Compare a similar addition to the divine prohibition in Genesis 2:17 and 3:3.

50. The master of riddles was completely unaware that the Lord possessed knowledge concerning Samson that the Danite himself did not perceive.

51. Joseph Blenkinsopp, "Some Notes on the Saga of Samson and the Heroic Milieu," *Scripture,* II (1959), 84.

52. Johannes Hempel, "Pathos und Humor in der israelitischen Erziehung," in *Von Ugarit nach Qumran* (BZAW, 77; Berlin: A. Töpelmann, 1958), 63–81.

53. Hermann Gunkel, "Simson," in *Reden und Aufsätze* (Göttingen: Vandenhoeck & Ruprecht, 1913), 44, writes that all animals are sad after coitus *(omne animal post coitum triste).*

54. K.R.R. Gros Louis, "The Book of Judges," *Literary Interpretations of Biblical Narratives* (Nashville: Abingdon, 1974), 159–160 calls attention to reversal of expectations in the Samson saga. He lists the following examples of peripeteia: (1) a barren mother expected no children; (2) readers expect a different kind of judge on the basis of the divine announcement; (3) Samson's parents did not expect Samson to marry a Philistine; (4) Samson expected to win his wager; (5) the Timnite's family did not expect Samson to return for her; (6) Samson did not expect Delilah to betray him; and (7) Philistines who summoned Samson to make sport for them did not expect him to kill them.

55. John McKenzie remarked, tongue-in-cheek, to be sure, that "The presence of three thousand people on the roof of such a building would have brought it down without any push from Samson" (*The World of the Judges,* 157).

56. Pedersen, *Israel,* III-IV, 46; Roland de Vaux, *Ancient Israel* (New York: McGraw Hill Book Company, Inc., 1961).

57. Martin Noth, "Das Amt des 'Richters Israels,'" *Festchrift Alfred Bertholet,* edited by Walter Baumgartner (Tübingen: J.C.B. Mohr, 1950), 404–417.

58. John Gray, ed., *Joshua, Judges and Ruth* (London: Nelson, 1967), 354.

59. "The commentators who have to prove Samson a blameless judge are much embarrassed by the Philistine women" (George F. Moore, *A Critical and Exegetical Commentary on Judges* (ICC; Edinburgh: T. & T. Clark, 1895), 318. John L. McKenzie, *The World of the Judges,* 158, writes: "As a popular hero Samson needs no explanation; as a charismatic hero he is hard to swallow."

60. Otto Eissfeldt, *The Old Testament* (New York: Harper and Row, Publishers, 1965), 257–267.

61. Gunkel, "Simson," 46, went so far as to consider the references to seizure by the spirit secondary.

Chapter Two
Passion or Charisma?

1. For details, see my essay, "The Samson Saga: Filial Devotion or Erotic Attachment?," *ZAW,* 86 (1974), 470–504.

2. Joseph Blenkinsopp, "Some Notes on the Saga of Samson and the Heroic Milieu," *Scripture,* II (1959), and Gerhard von Rad, "Die Geschichte von Simson," in *Gottes Wirken in Israel: Vorträge zum Alten Testament,* edited by O.H. Steck (Neukirchen-Vluyn: Verlag des Erziehungesvereins, 1974), 52. Whereas Blenkinsopp emphasizes the

broken vow, von Rad focuses upon Samson's squandered gifts. In the end Samson accomplished nothing, von Rad writes, and at last perished in the chaos that he had spread around himself.

3. No satisfactory solution to the problem caused by the number seven has been found.

4. How did Delilah know Samson had finally spoken the truth? A haggadic explanation points out that Samson's use of God in connection with the word Nazirite provided the decisive clue: Delilah knew he would never have lied in such a solemn context (Aaron Rothkoff, "Samson," *Ency Jud*, 14 [1971], 773–774).

5. John L. McKenzie, *The World of the Judges* (Englewood Cliffs: Prentice-Hall, 1966), 156, thinks Delilah was probably an Israelite, since she was able to communicate with Samson verbally, and Philistines would not have had to reward one of their own.

6. The author of Proverbs 6:27–28 phrased the problem of associating with a harlot another way: "Can a man carry fire in his bosom and his clothes not be burned? Or can one walk upon hot coals and his feet not be scorched?"

7. Josephus, *Antiquities of the Jews,* vol. 5, trans by H. St. J. Thackeray and Ralph Marcus, 9 vols., Cambridge: Harvard U. Press, 1950. § 279 emphasizes Manoah's jealousy because of his wife's glowing description of the angel, which evoked suspicion of wrongdoing on her part.

8. Gerhard von Rad, *Moses* (London: Lutterworth Press, 1959), 22–23, interprets Manoah's persistence as an effort to make use of the divine power for his own ends.

9. The angel refers to his name as wonderful *(peli'),* whereupon Manoah offers a *minchah* sacrifice to the One working wonders *(maphli').* The textual problem is hardly solved by Boling's restoration of the divine name from LXX[AL]. I do not find a chiastic structure in the text, even granting the restoration *(Judges* [AB,6] [New York: Doubleday, 1975], 222). The angel's choice of terminology recalls a similar passage, Genesis 18, where the same root occurs ("Is anything too wonderful for the Lord . . . ?").

10. "It is Samson's mother who first perceives that God's revelation, despite its awesome Otherness, contains within it the assurance of God's love" (Shalom Carmy, "The Sphinx as Leader: A Reading of Judges 13—16," *Tradition,* 14, No. 3, 75).

11. For a different view, see H.W. Hertzberg, *Die Bücher Josua, Richter, Ruth* (ATD, 9; Göttingen: Vandenhoeck and Ruprecht, 1959), 229; K. Budde, *Das Buch der Richter* (KHCAT, 7; Freiburg: J.C.B. Mohr, 1897), 98, who asks whether *'ishah* connotes a widow or a divorcee, and is contemptuous. Incidentally, Delilah is also designated an *'ishah.*

12. Edmund Leach, *Genesis as Myth and Other Essays* (London:

Jonathan Cape, 1969), 25–83, exaggerates the role of the conflict between endogamy and exogamy in Israel's traditions.

13. Gustav Boström, *Proverbiastudien* (Lund: C.W.K. Gleerup),
1935.

14. Gerhard von Rad, *Wisdom in Israel* (Nashville: Abingdon Press,
1972), 240.

15. On this personification of wisdom (and folly), see Bernhard Lang,
Frau Weisheit (Düsseldorf: Patmos Verlag, 1975).

16. Abraham Malamat, "The Period of the Judges," in *The World
History of the Jewish People*, vol. 3, ed. by Benjamin Mazar (Tel Aviv:
Rutgers University Press, 1971), 129–163.

17. On the absence of Samson's mother during this journey, Carmy
writes: "While the mentioning of the father without the mother is not,
in itself, exceptional, in this case, after both father and mother are
repeatedly mentioned, the omission of the mother is reason for analysis" ("The Sphinx as Leader: A Reading of Judges 13—16," 79).

18. For analysis see my essay, "Journey into Oblivion: A Structural
Analysis of Gen. 22:1–19," *Soundings* (Nashville: The Society for Religion in Higher Education, Vanderbilt University), 58 (1975), 243–256.

19. All quotations of Milton's *Samson Agonistes* are taken from A.E.
Barker, ed. *John Milton: Samson Agonistes and Shorter Poems* (New
York: Appleton-Century-Crofts, Inc.), 1950.

20. I have discussed this theme with reference to 1 Kings 13 in
Prophetic Conflict (BZAW, 124; Berlin: Walter de Gruyter, 1971), 39–
49.

21. The error arose from the similarity between the two words, *ra'ah*
(to see) and *yare'* (to fear).

22. Rembrandt's painting of Samson threatening his father-in-law
immediately comes to mind (Berlin Museum).

23. A. van Selms, "The Best Man and Bride—from Sumer to St. John
with a New Interpretation of Judges, Chapters 14 and 15," *JNES*, 9
(1950), 65–75.

24. "They are afraid to attack him, even when it might be presumed
that he was scarcely in a position to defend himself quickly" (John L.
McKenzie, *The World of the Judges* [Englewood Cliffs: Prentice-Hall,
1966], 155).

25. Arvid S. Kapelrud, *The Violent Goddess. Anat in the Ras
Shamra Texts* (Oslo: Universitetsforlaget), 1969.

26. Sota 9b. Sota belongs to the third division of the Mishnah; the
title of this division is Nashim (Women). See Herbert Danby, *The
Mishnah* (London: Oxford University Press, 1933), pages 293–307 for
discussion of women suspected of adultery. To quote page 294, "Samson went after [the desire of] his eyes—therefore the Philistines put
out his eyes. . . ."

27. According to an haggadic text, Philistine women came to Samson in prison hoping to have giant children by him (Gustav Rothkoff, "Samson," *Ency Jud*, 14 [1971], 773). Ludwig Levy, "Sexualsymbolik in der Simsonsage," *ZS*, 3 (1916) exaggerates the sexual symbolism within the story of Samson.

28. Are we to conclude that the Philistines were so stupid that they allowed Samson's hair to grow once more?

29. Bertil Albrektson, *History and the Gods* (Lund: C.W.K. Gleerup, 1967), corrects the tendency among scholars to emphasize Israel's distinctive salvation history.

30. *sachaq* and *tsachaq*.

Chapter Three
The Riddles

1. Karl Budde, "Samson," *Hastings' Dictionary of the Bible* (New York: Charles Scribner's Sons, 1902), 380.

2. On riddles, see André Jolles, *Einfache Formen* (Tübingen: Max Niemeyer Verlag, 1968), 126–149 (original publication, 1930); Mathilde Hain, *Rätsel* (Stuttgart: J.B. Metzlersche Verlagsbuchhandlung, 1966); Archer Taylor, *The Literary Riddle before 1600* (Cambridge: University Press, 1949); Aug. Wünsche, *Die Räthselweisheit bei den alten Hebräern* (Leipzig: Otto Schulze, 1883); E. Ruoff, *Arabische Rätsel* (Tübingen Diss.), 1933.

3. Jolles, *Einfache Formen*, 126–149.

4. I have devoted considerable energy to restoring biblical riddles now in disintegrated form, and hope to publish the results of this research in due time.

5. For an attempt to recover riddles in a given text, see Leo G. Perdue, "The Riddles of Psalm 49," *JBL*, 93 (1974), 533–542.

6. See my article, "A Liturgy of Wasted Opportunity (Am. 4:6–12; Isa. 9:7—10:4; 5:25–29)," *Sem*, 1 (1970), 27–49.

7. Hans-Peter Müller, "Der Begriff 'Rätsel' im Alten Testament," *VT*, 20 (1970), 465–489; "Magisch-Mantisch Weisheit und die Gestalt Daniels," *Ugarit-Forschungen*, 1 (1969), 79–94.

8. Solomon Schechter, "The Riddles of Solomon in Rabbinic Literature, *Folklore*, 1 (1890), 349–358; Moses Gaster, "The Story of Solomon's Wisdom," *Folklore*, 1 (1890), 133–135; W. Hertz, "Die Rätsel der Königen von Saba," *ZDA*, 27 (1883), 1–33; Theodor Zachariae, "Rätsel der Königen von Saba in Indien," *ZVV*, 24 (1914), 421–424; Edward Ullendorff, *Ethiopia and the Bible* (London: Oxford University Press, 1968).

9. Cited from E.I. Gordon, *Sumerian Proverbs* (Philadelphia: The University Museum, University of Pennsylvania, 1959), 1.

10. Norman C. Habel, "The Symbolism of Wisdom in Proverbs 1—9," *Inter*, 26 (1972), 131–157.

11. On this contest (1 Esdras 3:1—5:6), see William R. Goodman, Jr., "A Study of I Esdras 3:1—5:6," unpublished Ph.D. diss., Duke University. I plan to publish an analysis of this text from the perspective of aesthetic criticism shortly.

12. Wünsche, *Die Räthselweisheit bei den Hebräern*, 61–62.

13. Josephus, *Antiquities*, V, 8¶6.

14. George F. Moore, *A Critical and Exegetical Commentary on Judges* (Edinburgh: T. & T. Clark, 1895), 335; C.F. Burney, *The Book of Judges* (New York: KTAV, 1970), 361; original publication, 1918.

15. Stith Thompson, *The Types of the Folktale* (Helsinki: Academia scientiarum fennica, 1928), 851.

16. Hugo Gressmann, *Die Anfänge Israels*, I (SAT; Göttingen: Vandenhoeck and Ruprecht, 1922), 243.

17. H.W. Hertzberg, *Die Bücher Josua, Richter, Ruth* (Göttingen: Vandenhoeck & Ruprecht, 1954), 230; Otto Eissfeldt, "Die Rätsel in Jdc 14," *ZAW*, 30 (1910), 132–135.

18. "Has she become pregnant without intercourse? Has she become fat without eating?" (W.G. Lambert, *Babylonian Wisdom Literature* [Oxford: Clarendon Press, 1960], 247). See also Hans Schmidt, "Zu Jdc 14," *ZAW*, 39 (1921), 316, and cf. Hosea 4:10.

19. Otto Eissfeldt, "Die Rätsel in Jdc 14." *ZAW* 30 (1910), 135.

20. Gordon, *Sumerian Proverbs*, 60–62.

21. J.R. Porter, "Samson's Riddle: Judges XIV. 14, 18," *JTS*, 13 n.s. (1962), 106–109; see also H. Bauer, "Die Rätsel des Simson," *ZDMG*, 66 (1912), 473–474; Harry Torczyner (Tur-Sinai), "The Riddle in the Bible," *HUCA*, 1 (1924), 125–149, especially 134. Heinrich Margulies, "Das Rätsel der Biene im Alten Testament," *VT*, 24 (1974), 56–76, postulates a mythological background for the riddle.

22. Torczyner, "The Riddle in the Bible," 133.

23. *ANET*, 426.

24. *ANET*, Sup, 643.

25. Although the metaphor itself may refer to choice cattle of Bashan, the use to which Amos puts it is certainly derogatory.

26. Wünsche, *Die Räthselweisheit bei den Hebräern*, 42–43.

Chapter Four
The Tragic Dimension

1. Hermann Gunkel, "Simson," in *Reden und Aufsätze* (Göttingen: Vandenhoeck and Ruprecht, 1913), 43, and Levy, "Sexualsymbolik in der Simsonsage," *Psychoanalytische Interpretationen biblischer Texte*, ed. by Yorick Spiegel (München: Chr. Kaiser, 1972), 88.

2. A haggadic homily has Samson utter these dying words: "O Mas-

ter of the Universe, vouchsafe unto me in this life recompense for the loss of one eye. For the loss of the other I will wait to be rewarded in the future" (Aaron Rothkoff, "Samson," *Ency Jud*, 14 (1971), 774.

3. Note the clever play on words here *(wayya'amidu* and *ha'ammudim).*

4. I do not use the word fate in its weighty sense, but think in terms of Qoheleth's use of *miqreh.*

5. von Rad, Gerhard, *Old Testament Theology* Vol. 1 (New York: Harper & Brothers, 1962), 325.

6. A similar theme occurs in the Book of Esther, where the wicked Haman's every action draws him ever nearer the gallows he has erected upon which to hang his foe, Mordecai.

7. Joseph Blenkinsopp, "Structure and Style in Judges 13—16," *JBL,* 82 (1963), 67.

8. Blenkinsopp in "Some Notes on the Saga of Samson and the Heroic Milieu," *Scripture,* 11 (1959), 81–89, reaches a different conclusion. He thinks the broken vow constitutes the "dynamic key-idea" of the story, which concerns a threefold violation of the nazir vow (eating honey from the lion's carcass; the feast at Timnah; and revealing his dedication to Yahweh and subsequent loss of hair). To this central notion has been added the motif of a "strong man helpless before the wiles of a woman," resulting in a unified narrative (84). See Blenkinsopp, "Structure and Style in Judges 13—16," 65–76 for further elaboration, especially in regard to rhythmic patterns and formulaic expressions.

9. Edwin M. Good, *Irony in the Old Testament* (Philadelphia: Westminster Press, 1965), 196, labels this belief a "magical assumption" that "has always pervaded human life."

10. See Patrick D. Miller, *The Divine Warrior in Early Israel* (Cambridge, Mass.: Harvard University Press), 1973.

11. Gerhard von Rad, *Moses* (London: Lutterworth Press, 1959), 22.

12. In his case we have to do "only with the involuntary uprising of a subject people against the alien and unloved oppressor, with little 'pin-pricks,' each of which is regarded as a heroic deed and greeted with malicious joy. But ten hot-blooded and foolhardy Samsons would not have been able to loosen the chains of Israel's bondage" (Karl Budde, "Samson," *Hastings' Dictionary of the Bible,* vol. 4, 379).

13. Shalom Carmy, "The Sphinx as Leader: A Reading of Judges 13 —16," *Tradition,* 14, No. 3, 66–67.

14. C.F. Kraft, "Samson," *IDB,* vol. 4, 200, and Gerhard von Rad, "Die Geschichte von Simson," *Gottes Wirken in Israel: Vorträge zum Alten Testament,* edited by O.H. Steck (Neukirchen-Vluyn: Verlag des Erziehungsvereins, 1974), 52, view Samson solely in terms of a negative example, as did Martin Luther.

15. Josephus, *Antiquities,* V, 317.

16. F. Michael Krouse, *Milton's Samson and the Christian Tradition*

(Princeton: University Press, 1949), 36–38. For much of what follows I am indebted to this work. See especially pp. 40–45, 51–52.

17. Thomas Hayne, *The General View of the Holy Scriptures*, (London, 1640), 217–218; in Krouse, *Milton's Samson and the Christian Tradition*, Plate III.

18. Krouse, *Milton's Samson and the Christian Tradition*, 34.

19. Krouse, *Milton's Samson and the Christian Tradition*, 71.

20. This quotation derives from John Lydgate's English paraphrase of Laurent de Premierfait's French version of Boccaccio's *De Casibus Virorum Illustrium* in *Fall of Princes*, 1, 3, 8, edited by Henry Bergen (London, 1924); and in *Troy Book*, 1, edited by Henry Bergen (London, 1906). See Krouse, *Milton's Samson and the Christian Tradition*, 60.

21. Marjorie Nicholson, *John Milton* (New York: Noonday Press, 1963), 363.

22. *Ibid.*, 361.

23. *Ibid.*, 364.

24. *Ibid.*, 351.

25. *Ibid.*, 357.

26. *Ibid.*, 354.

27. Anthony Low, *The Blaze of Noon: A Reading of Samson Agonistes* (New York and London: Columbia University Press, 1974), offers numerous insights into the tragedy that, apart from Shakespeare's, "is unequaled by any other English tragedy in the strength of its emotions, the authority of its action, the quality of its verse, or in sheer total density" (vii). Low thinks the work fuses Christian and classical themes, and argues for a late date largely because of its similarity to Milton's *Christian Doctrine*. He points to several tragic patterns within the poem, emphasizes irony and the image of sight versus blindness, and discusses the importance of vengeance to the tragedy. Low counters the tendency to disparage Dalilah and Manoah, and praises the flexible poetic meter. Copious notes make this study indispensable for anyone interested in a critical understanding of *Samson Agonistes*.

Afterword: The Secret Is Out

1. Karl Budde, "Samson," *Hastings' Dictionary of the Bible*, vol. 4 (New York: Charles Scribner's Sons, 1902), 379.

2. Joseph Blenkinsopp, "Some Notes on the Saga of Samson and the Heroic Milieu," *Scripture*, 11 (1959), 83.

3. C.F. Burney, *The Book of Judges* (New York: KTAV, 1970), 337.

4. James A. Wharton, "The Secret of Yahweh: Story and Affirmation in Judges 13—16," *Inter*, 27 (1973), 66.

Selected Bibliography*

Alonso-Schökel, Luis. "Erzählkunst im Buche der Richter." *Bib* 42 (1961): 143–172.

_____. "Narrative Structures in the Book of Judith." *Colloquy* 2, Berkeley: Center for Hermeneutical Studies, 1975.

Auerbach, Erich. *Mimesis: The Representation of Reality in Western Literature.* Trans. by Willard R. Trask. Princeton: University Press, 1953.

Bauer, H. "Zu Simsons Rätsel in Richter Kapitel 14." *ZDMG* 66 (1912): 473–474.

Blenkinsopp, Joseph. "Some Notes on the Saga of Samson and the Heroic Milieu." *Scripture* 11 (1959): 81–89.

_____. "Structure and Style in Judges 13—16." *JBL* 82 (1963): 65–76.

Boling, Robert G., ed. *Judges* (AB, 6). New York: Doubleday, 1975.

Budde, Karl. *Das Buch der Richter* (KHCAT). Freiburg: J.C.B. Mohr, 1897.

_____. "Samson." In *Hastings' Dictionary of the Bible,* vol. 4. New York: Charles Scribner's Sons, 1902: 377–381.

Burney, C.F. *The Book of Judges.* New York: KTAV, 1970. First published, 1918.

Carmy, Shalom. "The Sphinx as Leader: A Reading of Judges 13—16." *Tradition* 14, No. 3 (1974): 66–79.

Carus, Paul. *The Story of Samson and Its Place in the Religious Development of Mankind.* Chicago: Open Court Publishing Company, 1907.

Cohen, A., ed. *Joshua and Judges.* London: Soncino, 1950.

Cohen, Gary G. "Samson and Hercules: A Comparison between the Feats of Samson and the Labours of Hercules." *EvQ* 42 (1970): 131–141.

Cook, Stanley A. "The Theophanies of Gideon and Manoah." *JTS* 28 (1927) Reprinted 1965, Wm. Dawson & Sons Ltd., London.: 368–383.

Cooke, G.A. *The Book of Judges.* Cambridge: University Press, 1918.

*Abbreviations used in this bibliography are listed on page 152.

Crenshaw, James L. "Journey into Oblivion: A Structural Analysis of Gen. 22:1–19." *Soundings* 58 (1975): 243–256.

――――. "Riddle." *IDB*, Sup. (1976): 749–750.

――――. "The Samson Saga: Filial Devotion or Erotic Attachment?" *ZAW* 86 (1974): 470–504.

――――. "Wisdom." In *Old Testament Form Criticism,* edited by John H. Hayes. San Antonio: Trinity University Press, 1974: 225–264.

van Dallen, Aleida G. *Simson.* Assen: Van Gorcum, 1966.

Diederichs, J.C.W. *Zur Geschichte Simsons: Richter XIV–XVI.* Göttingen: J.C. Dieterich, 1778.

van Doorninck, Adam. "De Simsonsagen: Kritische Studiën over Richteren 14–16." *ThT* 28 (1894): 14–32.

Eissfeldt, Otto. *Die Quellen des Richterbuches.* Leipzig: J.C. Hinrichs, 1925.

――――. "Die Rätsel in Jdc 14." *ZAW* 30 (1910): 132–135.

Feldman, Shammai. "Biblical Motives and Sources." *JNES* 22 (1963): 73–103.

Fensham, F.C. "The Judges and Ancient Israelite Jurisprudence." *OTWSA* (1959): 15–22.

――――. "The Shaving of Samson: A Note on Judges 16:19." *EvQ* 31 (1959): 97–98.

Gaster, Theodor H. *Myth, Legend, and Custom in the Old Testament.* New York: Harper, 1969.

Gese, Hartmut. "Simson." *RGG*[3] 6 (1962): 41–43.

Gray, John, ed. *Joshua, Judges and Ruth* (CB). London: Nelson, 1967.

Greenfield, J.C. "Philistines," *IDB* 3 (1962): 791–795.

Gressmann, Hugo. Die Anfänge Israels (SAT). Göttingen: Vandenhoeck and Ruprecht, 1922.

Gros Louis, Kenneth R.R., "The Book of Judges." In *Literary Interpretations of Biblical Narratives,* edited by K.R.R. Gros Louis, James S. Ackerman, and Thayer S. Warshaw. Nashville: Abingdon, 1974: 141–162.

Gunkel, Hermann, "Sagen und Legenden: II. In Israel." *RGG*[2] 5 (1931): 49–59.

――――. "Simson." in *Reden und Aufsätze.* Göttingen: Vandenhoeck and Ruprecht, 1913: 38–64.

Gunn, D.M. "Narrative Patterns and Oral Tradition in Judges and Samuel." *VT* 24 (1974): 286–317.

Hartmann, Richard. "Simsons Füchse." *ZAW* 31 (1911): 69–72.

Haupt, P. "Samson and the Ass's Jaw." *JBL* 33 (1914): 296–298.

Hertzberg, H.W. *Die Bücher Josua, Richter, Ruth* (ATD). Göttingen: Vandenhoeck and Ruprecht, 1954.

Humbert, Paul. "Les métamorphoses de Samson." *RHR* 80 (1919): 154–170.

Jolles, André. *Einfache Formen.* Tübingen: Max Niemeyer Verlag, 1972.

Kraft, C.F. "Judges, Book of." *IDB,* vol. 2, 1013–1023.

———. "Samson," *IDB,* vol. 4, 198–201.

Lagrange, Marie Joseph. *Le livre des Juges.* Paris: Librairie Victor Lecoffre, 1903.

Levy, Ludwig. "Sexualsymbolik in der Simsonsage." In *ZS* 3 (1916): 256–271. Also in *Psychoanalytische Interpretationen biblischer Texte,* edited by Yorick Spiegel. München: Chr. Kaiser, 1972: 75–93.

Lods, Adolphe. "Quelques remarques sur l'histoire de Samson." *RHP* 4 (1924): 493–503.

McKenzie, John L. *The World of the Judges.* Englewood Cliffs: Prentice-Hall, 1966.

Malamat, Abraham. "The Period of the Judges." In *The World History of the Jewish People,* 3, edited by Benjamin Mazar. Tel Aviv: Rutgers University Press, 1971: 129–163.

Margulies, Heinrich. "Das Rätsel der Biene im Alten Testament." *VT* 24 (1974): 56–76.

Mayes, A.D.H. *Israel in the Period of the Judges* (SBTh, 29). London: SCM, 1974.

Mazar, Benjamin, ed. "The Philistines and Their Wars with Israel." In *The World History of the Jewish People,* 3, *Judges.* Tel Aviv: Rutgers University Press, 1971: 164–179.

Moore, G.F. *A Critical and Exegetical Commentary on Judges* (ICC). Edinburgh: T. & T. Clarke, 1895.

Müller, H.P. "Der Begriff 'Rätsel' im Alten Testament." *VT* 20 (1970): 465–489.

Myers, Jacob M. "Introduction and Exegesis to the Book of Judges." *IB* II: 677–826.

Noth, Martin. "Das Amt des 'Richters Israels.' " In *Festschrift Alfred Betholet,* edited by Walter Baumgartner. Tübingen: J.C.B. Mohr, 1950: 404–417.

Nowack, Wilhelm. *Richter, Ruth und die Bücher Samuelis.* HKAT, 4. Göttingen: Vandenhoeck and Ruprecht, 1902.

Olrik, Axel. "Epic Laws of Folk Narrative." In *The Study of Folklore.* Edited by Alan Dundes. Englewood Cliffs, NJ: Prentice-Hall, 1965.

Porter, J.R. "Samson's Riddle: Judges XIV. 14, 18." *JTS,* n.s. 13 (1962): 106–109.

Propp, V. *Morphology of the Folktale,* Edited by L. Wagner. Translated by L. Scott. Second edition. Austin: University of Texas, 1968.

von Rad, Gerhard. "Die Geschichte von Simson." In *Gottes Wirken in Israel: Vorträge zum Alten Testament,* edited by O.H. Steck. Neukirchen-Vluyn: Verlag des Erziehungesvereins, 1974: 49–52.

Rauber, D.F. "Literary Values in the Bible: The Book of Ruth." *JBL*

89 (1970): 27–37.

Richter, Wolfgang. *Traditionsgeschichtliche Untersuchungen zum Richterbuch.* BBB 18. Bonn: Peter Hanstein Verlag, 1963.

Roskoff, Gustav. *Die Simsonssage nach ihrer Entstehung, Form und Bedeutung und der Heraclesmythus.* Leipzig: Ernst Bredt, 1860.

Rothkoff, Aaron. "Samson." *Ency Jud* 14 (1971): 771–777.

Rylaarsdam, J. Coert. "Nazirite." *IDB,* vol. 3 (1962): 526–527.

Scheiber, A. "Samson Uprooting a Tree." *JQR* 50 (1959): 176–180.

————. "Further Parallels to the Figure of Samson the Tree-Uprooter." *JQR* 52 (1961): 35–40.

Schlauri, Ignaz. "Wolfgang Richters Beitrag zur Redaktionsgeschichte des Richterbuches." *Bib* 54 (1973): 367–403.

Scholes, Robert and Kellogg, Robert. *The Nature of Narrative.* London: Oxford University Press, 1966.

Schunck, K.D. "Die Richter Israels und ihr Amt." *VTS* 15 (1965): 252–262.

van Selms, A. "The Best Man and Bride—from Sumer to St. John with a New Interpretation of Judges, Chapters 14 and 15." *JNES* 9 (1950): 65—75.

Simpson, C.A. *Composition of the Book of Judges.* Oxford: Blackwell, 1957.

Smythe-Palmer, A. *The Samson-Saga and its Place in Comparative Religion.* London: Sir Isaac Pitman and Sons, 1913.

Soggin, J. Alberto. *When the Judges Ruled.* London: Lutterworth Press, 1965.

Stahn, Hermann. *Die Simson-Saga: Eine religionsgeschichtliche Untersuchung.* Göttingen: Vandenhoeck and Ruprecht, 1908.

Steinthal, H. "The Legend of Samson." In *Mythology Among the Hebrews,* by Ignaz Goldziher. Translated by Russell Martineau. New York: Cooper Square Publishers, Inc., 1967: 392–446. Original publication by Longmans, Green, and Co., London, 1877.

Torcszyner, Harry (Tur-Sinai). "The Riddle in the Bible." *HUCA* 1 (1924): 125–149.

Weiss, Meir. "Einiges über die Bauformen des Erzählens in der Bibel." *VT* 13 (1963): 456–475.

————. "Weiteres über die Bauformen des Erzählens in der Bibel." *Bib* 46 (1965): 181–206.

Wharton, James A. "The Secret of Yahweh: Story and Affirmation in Judges 13—16." *Inter* 27 (1973): 48–66.

Wimsatt, W.K., Jr. and Beardsley, M.C. "The Intentional Fallacy." In *The Verbal Icon: Studies in the Meaning of Poetry.* Lexington: University of Kentucky Press, 1954: 2–18.

Zapletal, Vincenz. *Der biblische Samson.* Freiburg: Universitätsbuchhandlung, 1906.

Index of Scriptural References

Index of Hebrew Words